"I have gained so much from the study of Master Ni's works that a great change is being worked into my life. It is so hard to find words to express this, this great opening, this clarity and gentle-heartedness, strength of purpose - oh, it is so good to have this friend who writes these remarkable, astonishing, accurate and true books."
- Megan Fleming, Australia

"His (Hua-Ching Ni) books and message are helping me change my life at a very subtle, even paced rhythm. All that he says makes so much sense to me, not in my mind but in my 'gut.' I feel this is the reality of life itself."
-Lisette Tingesdahl, Janesville

"Thank you for teaching me through your books. They center me, lift me up, and sometimes bring a smile of happiness to my face. Reading them makes me feel clean and refreshed. As I walk along, experiencing one day after another, your books are a good friend and guide to me."
-Don Janus, Dallas

"This knowledge is a priceless treasure that I have been searching for for many years, from library to book store, but finally I've found them."   -Andre Luu, San Francisco

"I am reading your book and feel that I am coming home."
-Fleur Dalton Green, Santa Fe

"I have been reading Tao, the Subtle Universal Law and the Integral Way of Life for the last six weeks. I greatly appreciate your book; it has benefitted me so much. I now have a good opportunity to observe the subtle energies more so than ever before."
- Joanna Rose Bullard, Los Angeles

TAO

The Subtle Universal Law
And the Integral Way of Life

TAO

THE SUBTLE UNIVERSAL LAW
& THE INTEGRAL WAY OF LIFE

(SECOND EDITION)

Hua-Ching Ni

**TAO OF
WELLNESS**

PRESS

We wish to thank the Bildarchiv Foto Marburg in Marburg, West Germany, for the use of the photograph on the cover.

Tao of Wellness Press
An imprint of Sevenstar Communications, Inc.
13315 Washington Blvd, Ste 200
Los Angeles, California 90066

The paper used in this publication meets the minimum requirements of the American National Standard for Information Sciences Permanence of Paper for Printed Library Materials, ANSI 239.48-1984.

First printing	September 1979
Second printing	October 1980
Third printing	November 1982
Fourth printing	October 1985
Fifth printing	March 1993
Sixth printing	March 1995
Seventh printing	February 1998
Eighth printing	June 2003
Ninth printing	December 2008
Tenth printing	June 2019

Library of Congress Cataloging-in-Publication Data
Ni, Hua-Ching.
    Tao : the subtle universal law and the integral way of life / by Hua-Ching Ni = [Yu chou kan yin chih tao / Ni Hua-ch'ing shu].
    p.   cm.
    Parallel title and author statement also in Chinese.
    "Sixth printing"--Colophon.
    ISBN 0-937064-65-3 (alk. paper)
        1. Taoism Doctrines   2. T'ai chi ch'uan. I. Title.
BL1925. N5   1993   93-12497
299'.51444--dc20   CIP

To

one sensitive enough to perceive the operation of subtle law in his life. May these books serve as a reassurance of the subtle knowledge which he knows but cannot tell.

To

one willing to cultivate the high sensitivity to recognize the subtle law operating in any moment or event, with the hope of harmonizing with the subtle law which is the reality of a good, stable life.

To all readers,

According to the teaching of the Universal Integral Way, male and female are equally important in the natural sphere. This fact is confirmed in the diagram of *T'ai Chi*. Thus, discrimination is not practiced in our tradition. All of my work is dedicated to both genders of the human race.

Wherever possible, constructions using masculine pronouns to represent both sexes are avoided. Where they occur, we ask your tolerance and spiritual understanding. We hope that you will take the essence of my teaching and overlook the limitations of language. Gender discrimination is inherent in English. Ancient Chinese pronouns do not differentiate gender. I wish that all of you will achieve yourselves well above the level of language and gender.

Thank you, H. C. Ni

Warning - Disclaimer

This book is intended to present information and techniques that have been in use throughout the Orient for many years. This information and these practices utilize a natural system within the body; however, no claims are made regarding their effectiveness. The information offered is according to the author's best knowledge and experience and is to be used by the reader at his or her own discretion and liability.

Because of the sophisticated nature of the information contained within this book, it is recommended that the reader also study the author's other books for a broader understanding of energy-conducting exercises and a healthy lifestyle.

People's lives have different conditions and their growth has different stages. Because the background of people's development cannot be unified, there is no single practice that can be universally applied to everyone. Thus, it must be through the discernment of the reader that the practices are selected. The adoption and application of the material offered in this book must therefore be the reader's own responsibility.

The author and publisher of this book are not responsible in any manner for any harm that may occur through following the instructions in this book.

Contents

The Teachings of the Integral Way *i*
Prelude *ii*
Preface *iii*
Introduction *v*

1. Energy: The Subtle Essence of All Creation 1
2. The Universal Energy Net 30
3. The Human Body and Universal Law 36
4. The Art of Preserving Health 53
5. T'ai Chi Movement, Universal Law and the Law of Individual Being 71
6. The Application and Practice of T'ai Chi Movement 77
7. A Simple and Practical Emotional Life 92
8. The Integral Science of Ethics 101
9. Spiritual Arts 109
10. The Mystical Changes in People of the Integral Way 141

Conclusion 144
Afterword 148
The Spiritual Background of Union of Tao and Man 150
Appendix: The Ancient Integral View of the Organs 156

List of Figures

1. Wu-Hsing, the Five Great Performers 9
2. The Solar Energy Cycle 11
3. The Five Phases of Energy Evolution 15
4. Correspondences of the Five Phases of Energy Evolution 16
5. Creative Order 17
6. Destructive Order 18
7. Competitive Order 19
8. The Daily Energy Cycle of the Channels 40

The Teaching of the Universal Way

as presented by Hua-Ching Ni

T   *stands for Truth*

A   *stands for Above*

O   *stands for Oneself*

Thus, Tao stands for
TRUTH ABOVE ONESELF.

Also,

T   *stands for Truth*

A   *stands for Among*

O   *stands for Ourselves*

Thus, at the same time, Tao stands for
TRUTH AMONG OURSELVES.

Prelude

The Subtle Essence conveyed by the teaching of the Universal Way is the deep truth of all religions, yet it transcends all religions, leaving them behind like clothing worn in different seasons or places. Religions wear out, but the ageless truth lasts through all changes. The teaching of the Subtle Essence includes everything of spiritual importance, yet it goes beyond the level of religion. It directly serves your life, surpassing the boundary of all religions and extracting the essence of them all.

The Subtle Essence as conveyed by the teaching of the Universal Way is also the goal of all sciences, but it surpasses all sciences, leaving them behind as partial and temporal descriptions and explanations of this universal Integral Truth. Unlike any partial science, the Way goes beyond the level of any single scientific search.

The Subtle Essence is the most central and creative teaching. It does not rely on any authority, nor does it build social authority. It is like a master key which can unlock all doors directly leading you to the inner room of the ultimate truth. It is not frozen at the emotional surface of life. It does not remain locked at the level of thought or belief with the struggle which extends to skepticism and endless searching.

The teaching of the One Great Path of the Subtle Essence presents the core of the Integral Truth and helps you reach it yourself.

Preface

The attainment and achievement of modern civilization is great in many areas, and modern inventions are undoubtedly useful tools for almost everyone. Unfortunately, human psychological life and the development of the individual personality have not made the same progress as modern technology, and their condition cannot be improved through modern inventions.

In the civilized western world, religion has been a dominant force in many aspects of life, with positive as well as negative results. Religion as a psychological "ruler" offers psychological strength to a person and assists him in dealing with daily problems. As science progressed, this psychological "ruler" became weaker in the lives of people with high intellectual development. This left their psychological life unprotected. Without universal guidelines for ethics and life in general, confusion arose with the appearance of many new ideas.

In the East, religion was not a ruling force, but more an art of psychological life and real spiritual achievement. However, because of fascination and obsession with material achievement, its previous attainment of psychological health and real spiritual achievement suffered a loss of attention and importance in modern life.

Surely, I do not mean the real importance of spiritual achievement and the plain truth of life has been lost. Yet the new situation of prosperity has not had much impact on the improvement of humanity's psychological health. In fact, it has been a detriment to real spiritual advance and brought some inconvenience to those who seek such development. Confusion is especially widespread among the younger generations in discovering ethical guidelines for daily use.

I struggle psychologically as well as spiritually along with the rest of humankind. The skepticism which grew out of my attraction to modern accomplishments brought me to thoroughly inspect the plain truth of life of ancient times to see if it was also the truth of modern life. Practically, the guidelines of the ancient ethics still hold true for modern people.

What I have to offer as an Integral healer and recognized Master of the Integral Way are the time tested systems of knowledge which were developed by ancient sages. The essence of this knowledge has helped my spiritual ancestors, myself and all the people I have treated and taught.

If one does not adhere to this wisdom, the results occur accordingly. The universal law of subtle energy response is just as accurate as modern technology, and it is effective in all interactions and transformations in the multi-universe.

In this book I present my training, cultivation and tradition, not to recommend anything, but rather for your earnest evaluation and with the hope that the reading may benefit and serve you in some way.

Hua-Ching Ni
November, 1979
Los Angeles

Introduction

"Fortune and disaster do not come through gates, but man himself invites their arrival." This statement expresses the universal law of subtle energy response as experienced by the ancient Masters of the Integral Way, the ancient achieved ones. The ancient Masters taught their students the universal law of response as the basis for all spiritual practices. This law reveals that energy of a specific vibrational frequency responds to and attracts energies of a corresponding frequency. Thus one's experience is determined by the energy one embodies. If one is in harmony with universal law, the manifestations of one's physical, emotional and mental energies will be harmonious. If one violates the laws of nature, one manifests disorder and disharmony in one's life. This work clarifies the nature of the universal law of energy response and explains its relationship to daily life and one's self-cultivation.

One must begin with the understanding that everything which exists in the universe is a manifestation of energy in grosser and subtler states. Everything in a particular environment is the manifestation of the energy of that environment. Fish, for example, are the manifestation of the energy of water, and are shaped differently depending on the warmth, depth and speed of the water. Insects in a garden are the manifestation of the energy of the garden, and so are the animals and vegetation which are found there. Humankind is the manifestation of the energies of the sun, moon, stars and other celestial bodies in the environment of the Earth. The energies of the celestial bodies in the astral world and all the energies of the immediate environment respond subtly to the energies of a human and influence the person directly. Each person is shaped by subtle and gross environmental factors, prenatal and postnatal conditions, and past lives or stages prior to this existence.

Prenatal conditions depend primarily on the condition of the parents' physical and mental energy at the time of conception and before birth. The energy formation of one's prenatal environment also includes the factors of geography and climate, the culture and customs of one's family and society, and one's location in relation to the energy rays of the celestial bodies and the rest of the universe. All of these ingredients generally influence the personality, character, propensities and fortune of an individual.

Postnatal conditions are the environmental influences after one's birth as well as one's experiences throughout the course of life. It is through the postnatal conditions that an individual has the possibility to choose to refine one's energy and engage in positive, constructive activities. By developing wholesome inner qualities, one may transcend one's own boundaries and fate. Postnatal conditions have two aspects: one is the influence of one's environment after birth; the other is one's reaction to and utilization of the elements of that environment.

The ability to adjust our external environment to suit our needs and aspirations is rather limited, and the destiny of the society we live in is generally beyond our direct control. What can be changed is the realm of one's own inherent energies, one's activities, the contents of one's mind, and the condition of one's spirit. Individuals with extremely good or extremely bad fortune are relatively few. The majority of humanity occupies the middle range, with great potential to alter the course of their lives by learning and adhering to the universal law which governs not only the affairs of humanity but the operation of the entire universe as well.

The events of one's daily life express all subtle influences and also reflect one's own energy. The interactions of this subtle energy network are far reaching and complex, and usually comprehended as destiny. Destiny, in actuality, is not determined by an external, divine authority. Rather it is the direct consequence of the energies which are held in body, mind and spirit of an individual as elements of personality. Subtle energy may be expressed by the conscious mind as ideas, concepts and behavior, or through the unconscious mind as subtle impressions absorbed through the senses. The frequency of energy radiating from one's own mind and spirit creates an attraction for the universal energies of corresponding frequencies, which invariably echo back as the ingredients of one's own daily experience. This principle is the basis for all spiritual practices.

One section of this book deals with how one's thinking and behavior influence the events of one's life and suggests the kinds of behavior that will evoke a harmonious response from corresponding universal energies. These days people tend to resist the notion that they must behave appropriately in order to have a good life. That kind of admonition is considered platitudinous and dogmatic. Actually, a good life is not a matter of doing right or wrong or of being good or bad; it is a matter of either maintaining in one's life the appropriate order of positive, harmonized energy or of violating it.

This understanding is essential for anyone who wants to experience the peace and contentment of a life in harmony with nature. It is especially vital for a spiritual student with highly developed sensitivity, because it is through the employment of the law of response and attraction of energy that one can experientially prove for oneself the subtle, universal reality which otherwise is only theoretical knowledge. Without the fundamental comprehension and application of the universal law, attempting to develop high spiritual understanding and attainment would be like building a castle on quicksand.

Among all of the precious rewards of life, inner peace is the most worthy. Of all eminent spiritual achievements, the attainment of a tranquil being is the most essential core of spiritual growth. In comparison to the universal principle of harmony and clarity, the highest arts of magic, the most dramatic of miracles, or the most eloquent spiritual messages are merely seduction, nothing more than obstacles to the maturity of one's spirit. This is why the ancient achieved ones or Masters traditionally rebuked any false authority beyond pure spirit itself. Following only the pure spirit, one never accepts any secondary descriptions or ornamentations of reality. The highest achievement as a spiritually developed person is the refinement of one's spirit into an irresistible precious sword which can cut through all mental obstacles and impediments. When one has achieved this level of refinement, there is nothing which can disturb the clarity and harmony of one's being.

Through following the principles of absolute mindedness and appropriate behavior and through the unfolding of one's own true character, one can increase the positive and harmonious response of the corresponding universal energies in one's daily life. It is the purpose of this work to convey to those who seek the truth the methods through which they may not only favorably reshape their daily lives, but also utilize the universal law of response and attraction of subtle energy to advance their own spiritual evolution.

The knowledge presented in this book is not something which can be grasped with one superficial reading. At first, it may seem obscure and difficult to understand, but through reflecting upon it and applying it practically in daily life, its deep meaning will gradually unfold. It may take one's whole lifetime to fully understand and realize these principles as experienced by the ancient developed people.

An undistorted human life is the real model of all universal truth. Sometimes we need to search for it in all dimensions. However, the external exhibition and discovery of truth is merely the reflection of its unfolding within, and likewise the internal recognition of truth displays itself externally.

Chapter 1

Energy
The Subtle Essence of All Creation

Vital energy or chi, as the ancient developed ones in the Integral Way referred to it, is formless, elusive and without tangible qualities, yet it is the subtle breath of life which permeates and vivifies the entire universe. We live in an environment of energy which envelopes and permeates us. Just as a fish is unmindful of the fact that it lives in water, we too are unaware of the vast, inexhaustible sea of energy which supports our lives. Chi gives birth to life; it is the generative force of the whole universe. The natural environment functions as the cosmic womb in which all manifestations of the universe are conceived and brought forth. Everything that exists in the universe is a manifestation or projection of that energy, in grosser or finer states, higher or lower frequencies of vibration. In order to gain mastery over our lives, it is necessary to have a basic understanding of the nature of energy and the cosmic principles of energy manifestation which influence us.

The principles which govern the energy formations and activities of the universe as a whole are the same principles which apply to any single part of the universe. From the smallest cell or atomic particle described in biology or physics, to the events of human history, even to the movement of the galaxies through space, all existence is regulated by the same cosmic principles. This includes all things regardless of their degree of completeness or incompleteness, or whether they die or exist eternally. Thus, by understanding the cycles of energy movement and evolution which occur both internally and externally, we gain insight into the very nature of the entire universe. By the same token, through studying the nature of the external universe, we gain insight into our own true nature. By familiarizing ourselves with the laws of nature, we may reconnect with our own true nature and thereby attract and evoke the response of positive universal energy.

Ancient sages described the movement and cyclic phases of energy evolution through the polar combination of yin and yang and the wu-hsing. The yin/yang system provides a basis for the analysis of all phenomena into complementary groups. The wu-hsing, which is frequently referred to as the five element system or the five forces is a schema used to describe cyclic processes into five temporally and qualitatively distinct parts.

Yin and Yang

> *Yin/yang is the Way of Heaven and Earth, the fundamental principle of the myriad things, the father and mother of change and transformation, the root of inception and destruction.* (Su-Wen)[1]

The original energy of the universe is fathomless and incomprehensible. It is beyond time and beyond space. Contained within it is all existence and non-existence. Yet it is neither existence nor non-existence. The ancient sages in one region of the world named it Tao. Tao, as the Subtle Origin of the universe, brings forth all things, nurtures and sustains them, and then draws them back to return to their subtle source. The ancient achieved ones revealed the subtle truth that the universe has two apparent aspects. One is the unmanifest aspect - the undivided oneness or ultimate nothingness, said to exist "before Heaven and Earth were born." In this aspect, the primal energy of the universe is undifferentiated, absolutely whole and complete. The other aspect is the manifest, perceptible world of multiplicity

---

[1] The *Yellow Emperor's Internal Book* is the collection of ancient life knowledge in relationship to nature. it contains two parts: *Su Wen*, the first part, describes the natural foundation of life. *Ling Shu*, the second part, discusses knowledge specific to acupuncture. *Su Wen*, as the foundation, covers a broader scope.

which is "after Heaven and Earth were born." Although these aspects appear as two, the manifest and the unmanifest are in fact one.

Tao manifests itself through an active process of self-expression. Creation may be viewed as the process in which the organization of the undifferentiated primal energy occurs. This organization brings about a polarization of the primal energy into two distinct categories called yin and yang. Although the active aspect (yang) occurs first, its presence implies the possibility of a relatively static perspective (yin) from which the action may be perceived. It is impossible to directly experience or absolutely define the quality of an action (yang) in space. It can be perceived only in relation to a solidified perspective (yin) which coincides and corresponds with it.

As an example, let us take the shining of the sun, which may be considered the supreme manifestation of the yang aspect of the solar system. It is not possible to determine that the sun is emitting rays if these rays do not strike another object. If they strike another object, the rays may be perceived because of changes observed in the object. Any positive statement about the sun's rays depends upon the observations made with reference to the object. Thus the effect stimulated by an action (yang) is confirmed by the solidified, relatively static object (yin) which corresponds with the effect. Through this polarization of activity and form, the primal energy gives birth to the active pole of the cosmos (Heaven) and the substantialized pole (Earth). Where there is one pole there must also be the other.

The act of creation may be thought of as an expansion of the primal energy outward from a center. However, for organization to take place, there must also be a coinciding, counterbalancing, contractive force. If the forces of centrifugality (yin) and centripetality (yang) were not equally balanced, nothing could exist. The energy would either disperse itself into nothingness or disappear into the center. The critical balance of these two forces is illustrated by the model of the atom. If the tendency of the electrons to propel themselves away from the nucleus of the atom were not counterbalanced by the force of the protons to attract the electrons to the center, the atom would disintegrate. On a much larger scale, this principle functions to hold together the solar system and the galaxies of the universe.

The nature of yin and yang was first recognized by Fu Shi who is said to have lived between 6,000 and 8,000 years ago by some and by others his life is estimated between 3852-2738 B.C. The Yellow Emperor (2698-2598 B.C.) stated that "the universe is an expression of the interplay and alternation of the two activities of yin and yang." He formulated twelve principles which further elaborate upon this relationship and provide us with an explanation of the absolute laws of nature which govern the universe. These principles are:

1. *That which produces and composes the universe is Tao, the undivided oneness or ultimate nothingness.*

2. *Tao polarizes itself: yang becomes the active pole of the cosmos, yin becomes the solidified pole.*

3. *Yang and yin are opposites, and each accomplishes the other.*

4. *All beings and things in the universe are complex aggregates of universal energy composed of infinitely varying proportions of yin and yang.*

5. *All beings and things are in a dynamic state of change and transformation; nothing in the universe is absolutely static or completed; all is in unceasing motion because polarization, the source of being, is without beginning and without end.*

6. *Yin and yang attract one another.*

7. *Nothing is entirely yin or entirely yang; all phenomena are composed of both yin and yang.*

8. *Nothing is neutral. All phenomena are composed of unequal proportions of yin and yang.*

9. *The force of attraction between yin and yang is greater when the difference between them is greater, and smaller when it is smaller.*

10. *Like activities repel one another. The closer the similarity between two entities of the same polarity, the greater the repulsion.*

11. *At the extremes of development, yin produces yang and yang produces yin.*

12. *All beings are yang in the center and yin on the surface. Yang means the acive spirit, yin means the physical body. On other occasions, yang means apparent and yin means hidden.*

There is no facet of life to which the activities of yin and yang do not apply. Yin and yang express the polar aspects and inter-relationships of everything that exists in the universe. Yin and yang have no fixed, explicit definition, which makes the terms virtually untranslatable. Rather, they represent two broad categories of complements, which include the correspondences of negative and positive, destructive and creative, inert and active, gross and subtle, actual and potential. Initially, the terms were used to connote the influences of the moon and sun. Their meaning was naturally extended to include the shady and sunny slopes of a mountain, the northern and southern banks of a river, the dark and sunny seasons, the front and back sides of the body, and the complementary aspects of social groups, including the opposite gender.

Thus, the definition of yin and yang cannot be limited solely to specific entities or cosmological principles or forces. The general overall definitions of the terms are as follows: Yang represents the quality of activity and yin the quality of solidification. The qualities of yin and yang are relative and not absolute. What might be considered yang in relation to one thing may be considered yin in relation to another, and vice versa. Furthermore, there is always yin within yang and yang within yin.

Over the course of time, the terms yin and yang have acquired a wide variety of associations. Yang generally signifies completion or the accomplishment or conclusion of some operation actively initiated. It implies something inducing action or motion - a stimulus, whereas yin signifies something confirming and responding - a response.

The Su-Wen says, "That which moves is yang." Thus yang articulates something dynamic or live; yin signifies something reposing or static, something dying off or fading away. Yin as the counterpart of dynamic action corresponds to a static position at which dynamic phenomena appear substantiated or stabilized, thus becoming perceptible and able to be defined in space. It is only through response that we perceive stimulus.

Yang signifies something causing change. Perceptible change is the criterion that lets us infer that "action" has taken place. The yin quality describes something tending to transform a momentary phenomenon into a persistent one, it lets fleeting qualities endure and maintains them unchanged. Yang implies creation and generation, whereas yin nourishes and supports growth. Yang implies something developing and expanding. It implies action that tends to expand in all directions from its supposed point of origin, whereas yin signifies something contracting, closing in. Yang signifies something indeterminate and formless which is nevertheless causal and determining. Yin indicates something with perceptible, specific qualities with the potential to be organized and formed.

All the energy manifestations in the universe may be understood in terms of the combinations and interaction of yin and yang. When subtle, positive yang energies meet and connect with gross, negative yin energies, a new manifestation or phenomenon comes forth. On the cosmic scale, we say the Yang Heavenly energies mix with the Yin Earthly energies to create all life. This is the basic pattern of the activity and interaction of all universal energies.

To attain real understanding of this, a student needs to develop powers of insight or intuition. The ancient sages developed brilliant insight through their direct response to the external environment. They discovered that universal primal energy is the Subtle Origin of all manifest beings and things, and that in the sphere where the energy exists before taking form, there is nothing which can be described.

Correspondences of Yin and Yang

YIN	YANG
Earth	*Heaven*
moon	*sun*
autumn, winter	*spring, summer*
things female	*things male*
cold, coolness	*heat, warmth*
moisture	*dryness*
inside, interior	*outside, surface*
darkness	*brightness*
things small and weak	*things large and powerful*
the lower part	*the upper part*
water, rain	*fire*
quiescence	*movement*
night	*day*
the right side	*the left side*
the west and north	*the east and south*
the front of the body	*the back of the body*
(from chest to belly)	*(from head to tailbone)*
the hours between noon	*the hours between*
and midnight	*midnight and noon*
exhaustion	*repletion*
murkiness	*clarity*
development	*incipience*
conservation	*destruction*
responsiveness	*aggressiveness*
contraction	*expansion*

These correspondences can continue ad infinitum.

Universal Development

All possible combinations of yang and yin and their formations and functions are contained in the *I Ching* or *Book of
Changes and the Unchanging Truth*. The *I Ching* describes
the development of the universe numerically. One represents the Subtle Origin which is unnameable and beyond
time and space. It is omnipresent and eternal.

The first divisions of manifestation from the Subtle
Origin are represented by two, the duality of yang and yin
energies, symbolized by an unbroken or strong line for yang
—— and a broken or weak line for yin — —. According to
their development, yang and yin are divided into "minor or
young yang" == and "major or old yang" === , and "minor
or young yin" == and "major or old yin" == . Yet this is
still not sufficient to accurately describe the movement and
development of phenomena. The complete manifestation of
subtle energy movement unfolds in three to six stages, each
symbolized by one line. The top three lines or stages are
referred to as the "upper kua," the bottom three as the
"lower kua." Kua means symbol. The manifestation of the
subtle sphere as Heaven or subtle energy is yang === and
the manifestation of the gross sphere of Earth, or physical
energy, is yin ≡≡ . The integration of the duality of yang
and yin is called the T'ai Chi ◑ , which brings forth life.
A human is a model of T'ai Chi, with subtle energy manifesting as the mind and spirit, and physical energy as the body.

Three represents the trinity of yang and yin, and their
integration, the T'ai Chi. These are considered the "Three
Treasures" of the universe.

Four represents the four basic forces of the universe, all
variations of yang and yin. The strong force of the universe
was referred to as "major yang." The weak force was called
"major yin." The heavy force was called "minor yin" and the

light force was called "minor yang."[2] For a force to be strong does not necessarily indicate heaviness; nor does a weak force necessarily indicate lightness. It is possible for a force to be both light and strong, weak and heavy.

The harmonization of the four forces creates a fifth united force, another T'ai Chi. The fifth united force is the harmonizing force of the universe, a common field. The ancient sages called these five forces the "Five Great Performers" of the universe or wu-hsing, and symbolized them with five physical manifestations.

WU-HSING
THE FIVE GREAT PERFORMERS

(Figure 1)

---

[2]These may possibly relate to what modern physics terms as "strong nuclear force," "weak nuclear force," "electromagnetism" and "gravity."

Water symbolizes the strong force, which is characterized by aggregation, contraction, collection and condensation. Fire symbolizes the weak force, characterized by expansion, disaggregation, dispersion and dissipation. Wood symbolizes the light force, characterized by explosion and dynamism. Metal symbolizes the heavy force, characterized by gravity. All these forces interact and are united and harmonized by Earth, the neutral force.

Six is manifested in the "Six Chi" or "Six Breaths," which are applied in integral medicine to determine the stage of development of a disease. They are elucidated in China's great medical heritage named *San Han Luon*, a book written by Master Chahn Chun Jang. The six chi or stages of disease are: lesser yang ☲ , middle yang ☳ and elder yang ☵ in the yang group, and lesser yin ☶ , middle yin ☴ and elder yin ☱ in the yin group, with pure yang ☰ and pure yin ☷ representing the healthy condition. The six chi manifest in the energy transformations of the human organs and also in the environment as climatic influences on diseases: wind, cold, heat, dampness and dryness, and fire.

Seven represents the process of change and recycling.

Eight represents the "Eight Great Manifestations" which are Heaven ☰ , Earth ☷ , Water ☵ , Fire ☲ , Thunder ☳ , Lake ☱ , Wind ☴ and Mountain ☶ . The eight great manifestations generate sixty-four hexagrams with 384 lines which display all possible combinations of yin and yang. The creative force of the universe lies in the interplay of the yang and yin energies. Individually, yang ☰ and yin ☷ can theoretically be expressed in a motionless state by the arrangement of lines. Sole yang and sole yin, however, bring forth nothing.

The universal energy movement manifests in cycles. For example, the energy cycle used by the ancient sages to describe the daily movement of the sun is composed of twelve segments. One can similarly employ the concept of yang and yin to symbolize a general increase or decrease of energy. An increase in yang energy indicates a decrease in yin energy and vice versa.

The energy cycle with twelve segments also applies to the annual solar energy cycle and to the twelve directions. The summer solstice is symbolized as ☰ , the winter solstice as ☷ , the vernal equinox as ☳ , and the autumnal equinox as ☴ . South is symbolized as ☰ , north as ☷ , east as ☳ , and west as ☴ . The universal energy cycles are explained in more detail in the sixty-four hexagrams of the *I Ching*. Through the study of this ancient text, one may come to understand the supreme logic inherent in the principles which underlie all manifestations and relationships in the universe.

THE SOLAR ENERGY CYCLE

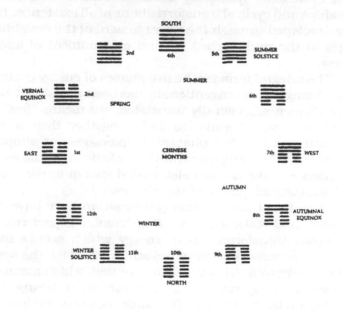

(Figure 2)

The Five Phases of Energy Evolution

The five phases of energy evolution, earth, metal, water, wood and fire encompass all phenomena of nature. It is a symbolism that applies itself equally to all life. (Su-Wen)

The evolution of the universe is not a linear process. Simultaneous with the expansion of the primal cosmic energy, its polarization and organization into interrelated cyclic patterns occurs. The ancient sages of the Integral Way used the function of yang and yin to describe the process of energy evolution and polarization. They discerned five interacting evolutionary phases or basic types of energy transformation, which they designated as earth, metal, water, wood and fire. This system provides a complete systematic symbology which illustrates the interrelationships and cyclical transformations of all existence. It too was developed through the direct insight of the enlightened sages in the undisturbed natural environment of ancient China.

The integral term for the five phases of energy evolution is wu-hsing which conventionally has been translated as the "Five Elements." Literally translated, wu means "five" and hsing as a verb means "to go." Together they may be translated as the "five phases" or "passages" or simply as "five to go." The designation of the evolutionary phases with the names of the natural elements does not imply a static and substantial quality of the phases.

The five types of energy transformation have both dynamic and static aspects. The dynamic aspect refers to the cyclic transformation of energy which occurs in the natural process of energy movement from which the system of time is derived. This is called wu-yuen, which means five phases of energy revolution. Literally yuen means movement or cyclic movement. The static aspect of the five basic types of energy transformation describes the typical quality of material things and is applied only as a classification.

Wu-hsing is the name given to this aspect, although wu-hsing is also the term used to refer to the five types of energy transformation in general.

One representation of the dynamic aspect is the yearly cycle of energy rotation occurring as the energy flows throughout the universe. One phase of this cycle is comprised of two years, with one year as its yang aspect and the other as its yin aspect. The complete cycle takes ten years, one shuen. In one decade the cycle traverses all five phases, following the creative sequence. The dynamic aspect is also seen in the daily and monthly cycles of energy rotation as well as in the corresponding energy cycles within the human body. Likewise, each phase or element can be viewed as either dynamic or static. The metal category, for example, viewed as dynamic, yields such actions as killing, battling, purifying and changing. Viewed as static, the metal category is exemplified by tools, implements and weapons. Illustrations of the dynamic aspect of the wood category are such climatic processes as wind, snowing, raining, thundering and lightning; whereas in its static aspect, the wood category is represented by trees, flowers and all kinds of vegetation.

The ancient spiritually achieved people understood wood as something pushing up, both in a straight or winding line. Metal meant something that is subject to change, fire something blazing upward, water something flowing down and earth something that can grow life. In their abstract meaning these elements can symbolize all substances or phenomena which in their nature contain the qualities displayed by the individual phases. The cyclic interaction of these elements can be employed to explain and to properly guide the interrelations of all substances and appearances in the universe, including man's internal and external world of experience. The five phases of energy evolution provide a complete philosophical and practical system which explains complex universal interrelations, and can be applied to reestablish disturbed energy arrangements and avoid conflicting situations.

The five phases of the cycle of energy evolution are linked, and they alternate in an unchangeable order. The interplay of these five transformations creates the macrocosm and is mirrored in the microcosm of a human being. Water and fire are the phases out of which life evolves, the metal and wood phases nourish life, and the earth phase is the neutral factor which supports life. The basic sequence of energy evolution is the productive or creative sequence called the "creative order." This is the yang cycle, which moves in a clockwise direction. In the creative order, each evolutionary phase generates the next in a continuously flowing movement. This is the cycle of birth in which each element is the mother of one element and the son of another. In this cycle the energy evolves from the water phase and transmutes to wood, fire, earth, metal and finally back to the water phase.

However, balance cannot be maintained with uncontrolled growth. Each phase must also control another and so keep growth within reasonable limits. Therefore, the second order of the cycles is the conquest or checking sequence referred to as the "destructive order." Each evolutionary phase in this cycle is considered to check the preceding one, thus counterbalancing the activity of the first sequence. This is the yin cycle, which also moves in a clockwise direction. In the destructive cycle, wood destroys earth, earth destroys water, water destroys fire, fire destroys metal, and metal destroys wood. The mutual breeding and conquering or subjugation of the various existing energies occurs simultaneously and without pause. It is this constant transformation of one phase into another which we call "life." These transformations never cease for one instant as the universe creates itself perpetually.

The third cycle of evolution is the "competitive order" in which the excess of one element results in the weakening and disturbance of another. Thus, fire competes with water, water with earth, earth with wood, wood with metal, and metal with fire. This cycle moves in a counterclockwise direction.

THE FIVE PHASES OF ENERGY EVOLUTION

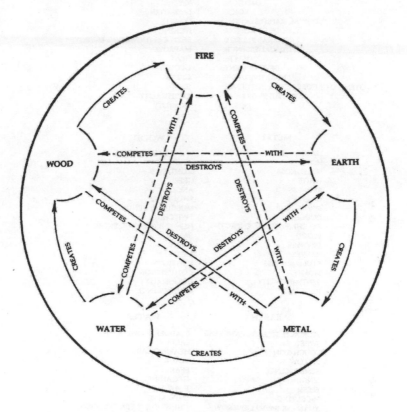

(Figure 3)

CORRESPONDENCES
OF THE FIVE PHASES OF ENERGY EVOLUTION

FIRE

ORGANS:	HEART, SMALL INTESTINE, PERICARDIUM, TRIPLE WARMER
FLAVOR:	BITTER
SENSE:	TASTE-TONGUE
COLOR:	RED
EMOTION:	JOY
VOICE:	LAUGHTER
PHYSICAL MANIFESTATION:	VESSELS
MODE OF ACTION:	ITCHING
INTERNAL ENERGY:	SHEN CHI (DIRECTING ENERGY)
PHYSICAL ESSENCE:	MARROW
CLIMATE:	HEAT
DEVELOPMENT:	GROWTH
NEGATIVE DRIVE:	GREED
POTENTIALLY CORRUPTING INFLUENCE:	SEX
ATTRIBUTES OF MIND:	SPIRITUALITY
MORAL:	HUMILITY

METAL

LUNGS, LARGE INTESTINE
HOT
SMELL-NOSE
WHITE
SADNESS
CRYING
SKIN & HAIR
COUGHING
PO CHI (PHYSICAL ENERGY)
BLOOD
DRYNESS
HARVEST
STUBBORNNESS
MONEY
SENTIMENTALITY
RECTITUDE

WOOD

LIVER, GALLBLADDER
SOUR
SIGHT-EYES
GREEN
ANGER
SHOUTING
MUSCLES & TENDONS
TWITCHING
HUN CHI (PSYCHIC ENERGY)
SALIVA
WIND
BIRTH
HOSTILITY
COMPETITION
RATIONALITY
BENEVOLENCE

EARTH

STOMACH, SPLEEEN/PANCREAS
SWEET
TOUCH-SKIN
YELLOW
REMINISCENCE
SINGING
FLESH
HICCUPING
YUAN CHI (PRIMAL ENERGY)
VITAL ESSENCE
HUMIDITY
MATURITY
AMBITION
MIND
TRANQUILITY
TRUSTFULNESS

WATER

BLADDER, KIDNEYS
SALTY
HEARING-EARS
BLACK
FEAR
GROANING
BONE
SHIVERING
CHING CHI (CREATIVE ENERGY)
SEXUAL ESSENCE
COLD
STORAGE
DESIRE
ALCOHOL
DESIRE
WISDOM

(Figure 4)

COMPETITIVE ORDER

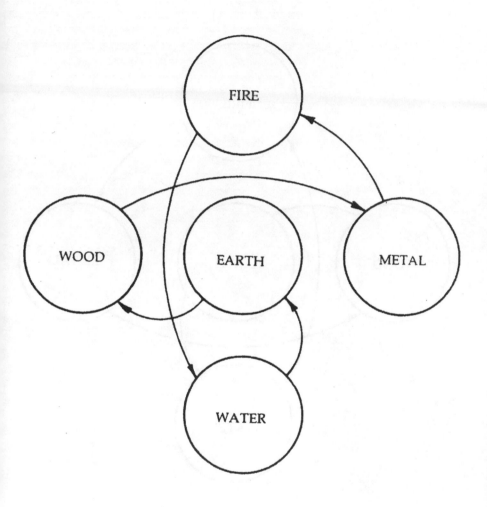

(Figure 5)

DESTRUCTIVE ORDER

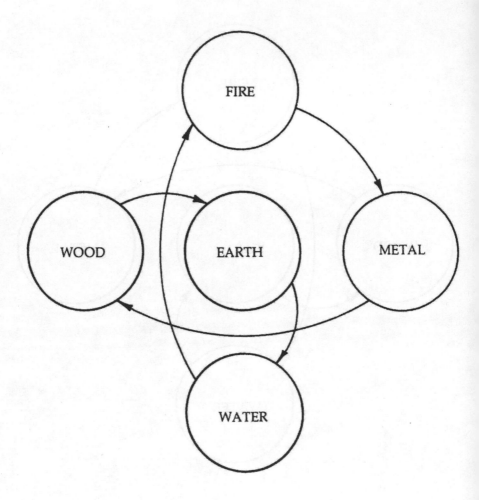

(Figure 6)

CREATIVE ORDER

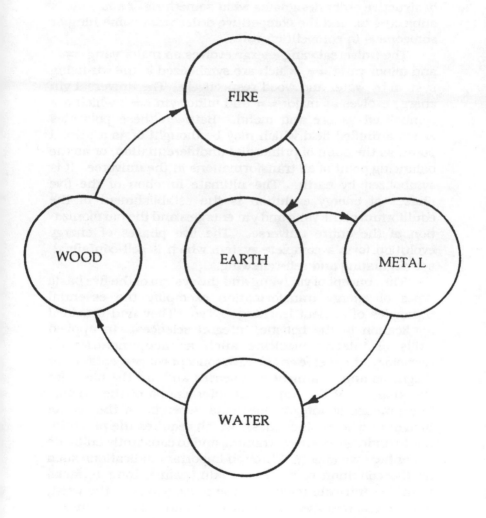

(Figure 7)

The creative order can be described more generally as that which can bring or has brought something about, or as what something or someone is receiving support from. The destructive order designates what something or someone is subjected to, and the competitive order what something or someone is in competition with.

The universal yang energy evolves as major yang ═══ and minor yang ══ which are symbolized in the wu-hsing system by water and wood respectively. The universal yin energy evolves as major ═ ═ and minor yin ═ ═ , which are symbolized as fire and metal. Between these polarities exists a unified field which may be thought of as a pivotal point, as the point of primordial undifferentiation, or as the balancing point of all transformations in the universe. It is symbolized by earth. The ultimate function of the five phases of energy evolution is the establishment of the equilibrium of the yang and yin energies and the harmonization of the entire universe. The five phases of energy evolution form a complete system which is self-contained, self-regulating and self-renewing.

The concept of yin/yang and the system of the five basic types of energy transformation exemplify the essential principles of ancient learning of Tao. They find practical application in the holistic, integral sciences. In applied skills of integral medicine such as acupuncture and herbology, they serve as effective concepts or perceptions for diagnosis and treatment of diseases and are the basis for the analysis of the functional interactions of the organs. The practice of integral medicine depends on the use of insight or whole-mindedness, which requires the practitioner to undergo extensive training and to constantly cultivate his or her own energy. Through important indications such as the condition of the eyes, skin, palms, tongue, facial aura, the intricate reading of the pulse waves at the wrist, and general inquiries about life style and habits, a comprehensive and integral view of the patient's health condition can be obtained. In this way, disturbances in the patient's energy system can be recognized before they manifest as acute symptoms, and the real causes of disease can be treated directly. While western medicine has reached high academic standards through laboratory work and modern technology, it hardly concerns itself with the treatment of disease in an integral way.

The yin/yang system and the five element system are also applied to explain the functions of mind and spirit and psychosomatic functions like the emotions. Mind and spirit are very subtle states of energy. When they materialize in the physical realm, they appear as phases of the five elemental qualities. Emotion is a heavier form of mental energy which can be expressed in various modes. Anger, for example, is a manifestation of the fire energy, sadness of the metal energy, and so on. When the emotions shift from one to another in response to the various stimuli throughout the day, the energy flows smoothly and health is maintained. When one particular emotion, however, is maintained as the keynote of one's mental composition, the creative cycle of the five elements is disrupted, the internal energies stagnate and disease manifests. This exemplifies the old adage that flowing water does not decay.

Other fields in which the concept of yin/yang and the five element system find application are political diplomacy, military strategy, agriculture, architecture, predictive sciences, and geomancy, which is the art of locating beneficial subtle energy rays geographically. The effectiveness of all traditional, integral knowledge stems from accurate insight and the understanding of the concept of yin/yang and the five basic types of energy transformation. Current scientific development, however, emphasizes analytic methods. This has fragmented the human mind and destroyed its capacity for direct, integral recognition and understanding. The utilization of insight is a precise metaphysical tool which, combined with the analytic capacity of the mind, enables humans to gain mastery over themselves and the environment.

The Principle of Energy Rotation

Following the subtle universal order revealed in the *Book of Changes and the Unchanging Truth*, we find that all of the manifestations in the universe adhere to the cosmic cycle of energy rotation. As it cycles, the energy of all universal manifestations undergoes specific stages of transformation. For the purpose of description, the great sages divided this universal cycle into twelve distinct sections and developed a system of twelve time-energy units which apply to all universal, yearly and daily cycles of energy transformation and evolution.

Everything in the vast universe has a time to be born, grow, ripen, mature and finally a time to fall, become latent and be reborn again. All physical existence follows this cycle of transformation, which has been designated by spiritually developed people as the "Heavenly Way of Rotation." Human civilization also has its life span, from its inception to the height of its development. When the peak of prosperity is reached, then it must decline and again come to darkness. Then the cycle continues and another new culture is born. The yearly energy rotation of the Earth demonstrates this cycle in the four seasons.

Similar to the yearly energy rotation of the Earth, the life of a human being follows its own cycle of energy rotation. The potential life span of a human being is 120 years. The first quarter of a person's life is the springtime of life, a time to grow and cultivate oneself. The second quarter corresponds with summer and is a time to develop and prosper. The third quarter of the cycle is the autumn of one's life, a time to harvest and enjoy the fruits of one's development. The winter quarter is a time to come back to quietness, to cultivate the vital root of life and to store one's energy. We need to engage in activities which are appropriate for the season of our lives. For example, when it is the spring of one's life, one should be active; when it is autumn, one should accept that it is autumn and develop mellowness of personality. However some people, in an attempt to physically prolong the spring-time of their lives, resort to artificial means such as the use of hormones to recapture their lost youth, which ultimately jeopardizes their health and well-being. The best policy is to follow what is natural and keep oneself in a natural condition without becoming disturbed by styles and fads in the external world.

The human life cycle may also be correlated with the daily rotation of energy expressed in the twelve two-hour segments of the solar energy cycle of time. The first stage corresponds with the period from midnight to morning. The second stage corresponds to the period from morning to noon. The third part of the cycle corresponds to the period from noon until evening. The last part of the cycle is the nighttime of one's life. All universal developments follow this cycle of energy rotation, whether it be the life of an individual, the rise and fall of a civilization, or the evolution of the galaxies. Everything with physical form is under control of the law of energy transformation. The only way for a human individual to transcend the cycle of transformation is through the complete spiritualization of one's being.

In the human realm, it is the energy rotation of an individual which forms a person's so-called destiny. The energy arrangement at the time of one's birth shapes the potential events of one's life. By calculating the five phases of energy evolution exhibited at the time of one's birth, beneficial or inauspicious times can be determined. This information can help one to plan one's life so as to be prepared for the hard times and to utilize the good times to their fullest potential. By understanding the cycles of one's life and of the universe, one can know the right time for any action. The highest code of ethics or morality is to abide by universal law. In this way one can keep pace with the unfolding of the universe and enjoy harmony with all existence.

Even though there may appear to be sameness, every manifestation of energy in the universe is unique unto itself and thus has its own particular natural order of development. For example, most flowers blossom in the spring or summer, but some, like the chrysanthemum, bloom in the frosty autumn. Plum flowers, the Chinese national flower, blossom in the winter. This is a result of the difference of energy manifestation. In the human realm, it is the different manifestations of energy of each individual which forms his or her own personal destiny.

Most people have formed the bad habit of looking outside themselves for external definitions of good or bad fortune, rather than considering the unique, natural order of their own development. They compare themselves to others and judge themselves by standards that are merely cultural inventions and which do not apply to the deep truth of their lives. If the flowers of their lives do not bloom according to an expected schedule or if they determine that the fruit of their lives is not as abundant as another's, they call it misfortune and feel troubled. They hope to do something to make themselves blossom earlier or to make their harvest seem greater. This is called "making an effort," and is against nature, against the personal nature of one's own unique development. Nature does not make critical value judgments of her precious offspring. The concepts of better or worse, sooner or later, are inventions of the mind which have been formed under the influence of one's culture. These concepts are unnatural.

Despite the fact that each manifestation is different in form and each energy rotation is unique in timing, the essential value of all things remains the same. In the relative realm, the human mind makes distinctions, evaluations and judgments. Yet at the depth of one's true nature, mental concepts dissolve and all that remains is the unconditional, essential nature of life. The only thing that keeps us from experiencing our essential oneness with nature is the critical mind. The sense of separation which results from being bound to the critical mind produces all our obstacles. It is the source of all our pain.

Energy in Daily Life
People tend to think that the events of their lives are determined by external influences. They may blame their

happiness of misfortune on a divine but external authority who arbitrarily imposes punishments and rewards upon them. Or they blame their mothers and fathers for either spoiling them or denying them the fulfillment of their early emotional needs. Perhaps they think it is their environment which is supportive or hostile toward them, or their racial or educational background which determines the joy or sorrow which enters their lives. Or maybe they feel that their lives are governed by blind chance. Generally, people tend to look no further than the superficial elements which compose their experience. They fail to realize the deep truth that what appears as external reality is actually only a mirror of their own inner consciousness.

It is the energy projected by an individual's own mind which creates his experience. Consciousness is the vessel. The events in one's life are merely the physical or mental manifestations of the vessel's contents. The events are thus nothing but reflected images of one's own mental energy. The secret to leading a positive life is to refine and harmonize one's energy so as to live in consonance with the order of the universe. Conversely, by holding negative energy in one's mind in the form of distorted thought patterns and attitudes, one's life will reflect negativity and disharmony.

Every facet of our being is a manifestation of energy. The human body is a complexly organized energy system comprised of physical materializations of the five phases of energy evolution. It is the vital energy or chi which enables blood to circulate, glands to secrete, and metabolic processes to take place. The presence or absence of the heartbeat is the indication used to determine whether a person is alive or dead, but what is it that determines whether the heart beats or ceases to beat? The heart beats because the vital energy dwells within the body. If the vital energy leaves us, the body becomes like a dry, empty shell devoid of life. It is not our outer form upon which our lives depend, but rather it is the subtle chi upon which our outer, physical form depends.

Generally speaking, because energy is so subtle, we are not aware that it circulates in our bodies throughout our individual energy network. Yet the physical organism is tangible and therefore observable. The physical state functions as a mirror in which we can perceive the condition of the subtler states of being, those of mind and spirit. Most of us tend to take harmony and balance for granted because everything flows so smoothly without any particular distinguishing event to stand out and grab our attention or annoy us. However, when our energy becomes disordered and symptoms of disease begin to show, we become aware that there is a problem. If, for instance, a woman has an energy disorder such as emotional depression, the disorder may express itself in problems with her menstruation. She may have cramps or headaches or her period may arrive late or be totally absent. Although she is probably unaware of the subtle factors involved, she will recognize that something is wrong because her menstruation is a tangible, integral part of her life.

When the subtle chi moves in the body, gross manifestations such as blood also move. Conversely, if the chi becomes imbalanced or its movement impeded, this will influence the balance of the glandular secretions as well as the circulation of the vital fluids in the body. There is an old proverb which states that "flowing water does not decay." This principle is equally true of energy. This is one of the fundamental principles of integral medicine and of the system of self-cultivation. When stagnation of energy and blood occurs and localizes, disease will appear. Cancer and ulcers are two of the many kinds of diseases which result from energy stagnation.

Engaging in strong emotion, either joy, sadness or any other emotion, can create imbalance and blockage in the energy network which, in turn, can cause the energy and blood in the related area to become stagnant or to explode in localized areas of the body. Emotion is a form of energy which creates the atmosphere in which our daily scenario takes place. When strong emotions arise in the mind, the peaceful order of one's energy circulation is disordered; tremendous energy is then generated in the body cavities, creating stress and pressure on internal organs. The heart and liver in particular are very fragile organs. They can become damaged easily from internal disorder and pressure caused by strong emotional excess. When a person becomes angry, the blood vessels of the head become congested. Should one of them be weak, it could rupture and bring on a stroke, or the negative energy which has risen to the head may be transformed into tears or obscene language. Emotional excess will damage the nerves and blood vessels, effecting poor blood circulation, imbalanced metabolism, and glandular dysfunction.

If, on the other hand, one's mental atmosphere is calm, healthy and positive, it will allow the energy in the internal network to flow normally and unimpeded. The practical value of keeping the mind quiet and poised is that in this way there is no undue emotional force to create stress and disorder in either the internal or external environment.

By practicing self-cultivation techniques, one develops a sensitivity to the energies constantly circling within the body. Descending downward from the top of the head is the frontal general yin channel called the jen mo. The energy swirls down the jen mo, then returns up the back of the body to the head by way of the general yang channel, the tu mo. Like water, the natural tendency of the gross yin energy within the body is to flow downward. If this internal energy leaks away through elimination or sex, or through what one consumes or what one produces, the end of life is accelerated. Health is endangered where there is lack of balance, self-discipline and personal concern. When the internal energy is controlled, like water being dammed, then it is guided through the energy channel like an aqueduct fulfilling the process of irrigation. The internal energy will naturally function to support the head and the spirit. This is the cyclic movement of the internal chi.

The strong drive in all living creatures to produce offspring is the result of the gross, physical energy flowing

downward into the reservoir of the sexual organs located at
the lowest level of the body's trunk. The refined yang energy
is said to be like fire, in that its natural tendency is to rise
upward. After undergoing refinement, the energy travels
across the perineum and ascends up the back to the head.
The lips function as the upper gate between the yin and
yang channels, with the anus functioning as the lower
gate.

When a person is born into this world, yin and yang
become distinguishable. The goal of spiritual cultivation is
to restore the oneness of the yin and yang energies through
unifying the jen mo and the tu mo once again to function as
one whole and continuous channel in the body's energy
system.

It is impossible to establish clarity and order in our
being unless our internal energies are in a state of harmony
and balance. By utilizing in our lives the same cosmic
principles which assure the harmonious functioning of the
universe itself, we can nurture our vital energy and establish the internal balance necessary for a happy life. The
principles treasured by ancient and modern sages are
simplicity, equilibrium, harmony and quietude. These
principles display the practical value of allowing one's
energy to evolve and function normally. By personifying
these cosmic principles, we come to realize that we embody
the entire universe. Microcosm and macrocosm become
one.

The *Tao Teh Ching* tells us that man follows the Way of
Earth, Earth follows the Way of all heavenly bodies, all
heavenly bodies follow the Way of the eternal Tao, and the
Tao follows its own nature. This is the principle of universal
order, the nature of the cosmos whose perpetual rhythm is
followed by all existence. Whether it be a single atom, the
human body, or the body of the entire cosmos, all energy
movement is essentially the same, always following the same
principles.

Differences among living beings arise as a result of the
degree of completeness of their energy systems. For

example, the energy systems of creatures lower than man on the evolutionary scale are generally more yin or more gross. Their degree of yang, or more subtle energy is relatively low. The human being holds the highest position in the earthly evolutionary scale because he embodies a balance of both yin and yang energies, both the physical and spiritual, the gross and the refined. Because it is potentially complete and balanced, the energy network in the human being is like that of the entire universe. Actually the internal channel system in the human body almost precisely mirrors the energy network of the universe.

It is only because we violate the natural equilibrium of the energy network of our being that we require self-cultivation as a remedy to bring us back to our integral state of evenness and balance. Most people develop only the physical aspect of their being, neglecting the spiritual because the pressures of living in society turn their attention away from the subtle truths of life. Thus their lives manifest imbalance and disharmony. The purpose of the esoteric process of the Integral Way is to refine the gross physical energy to the more subtle level of spiritual energy so that we may once again connect our being with the Subtle Origin of the universe. This is sometimes called embodying or realizing the universe within you body. It is not just an idea or a theory, but has actually been experienced by generation after generation of achieved ones.

The eternal Tao is the primal energy of the universe. If one engages in following this energy by embracing Tao and acting only as an expression of Tao, one can become integrated with the essence of all life. Then, as the *Tao Teh Ching* puts it: "Without going outside the door, one understands all that takes place under the sky. Without looking through the window, one sees the Way."

Chapter 2

The Universal Energy Net

The vibrational frequency of energy has its own specific channel whereby it is transmitted throughout the cosmos. All universal channels are interwoven, forming a subtle network which contains all existence within it. The mutual attraction of yin and yang energies throughout the entire universe creates the interweaving of this cosmic energy net. The universal energy network is somewhat similar to the vast and complex transportation system of a large modern city. Like the lanes of modern freeways, each energy channel has its own scope and range of activity. The channels of the subtle universal energy are omni-dimensional and resemble the ground states of electrons which orbit the nucleus of an atom.

If one violates the regulative order of an energy channel by violating cosmic law, the result is disharmony and dissolution. On the other hand, by following the natural order of the positive energy channels one may achieve harmony with the universe and manifest a healthy, fruitful life. Achieving harmony in one's life is like aiming an arrow at a target and precisely hitting the bull's eye. Discord, sickness and disaster are merely a matter of "missing the mark," or extending oneself beyond the appropriate course for one's own inherent nature.

The energy network of the universe is an inescapable net. It you touch a string of the energy net you will get a response. If you insistently construct your own energy net by holding fast to your emotions, desires, attachments and ideas, you become like the silkworm which spins out a cocoon, only to imprison itself. However, if you can transcend your own mind, you can avoid being trapped in its net. Then, although you are still living within the vast universal network, you will enjoy freedom of action and being because of the understanding and ability which you achieved.

In order to hit the bull's eye of one's subtle target which is the essential core of one's being, one must project the arrows of one's thoughts and actions with accuracy so that they follow the correct energy channels. The true, appropriate course is held within our own natures but we miss it in the confusion and distortion caused by mental conditioning. The course is obscured by our misunderstanding as a result of the incomplete development of our minds and spirits.

Before a human being enters the physical plane to become individualized, he or she resides in the cosmic womb of nature. In some respects this is analogous to the experience of being a fetus in the womb of one's physical mother. While contained within your mother's womb, you were one with her; whatever your mother experienced you also experienced. In the process of birth you became separated from your mother. Your direct connection with her was cut. Similarly, before being born into this plane, we were one with nature and thus with universal law. Yet when we take physical form, we appear to become separated from the cosmic mother; we seem to lose our oneness with the universe and its law. We see nature and universal natural law as separate and external to our own nature. In truth, this separation is only an illusion, but when we accept the illusion as true, we also accept the separation.

After being born into the physical plane, we must rediscover universal law and restore our innate spiritual ability. By so doing, we reestablish our direct connection with nature, the cosmic mother of the universe. The reason we are no longer one with universal law in the postnatal stage is that we individualize ourselves via the mind. We perceive everything in terms of subject and object. We see universal nature as something other than ourselves. Actually we are the universal energy and the universe is us. Now our sensitivity to the movement of the vast universe is limited because we have physical form. Yet we need only to break through the shell of the ego to realize that we are one with the universe and that our concepts of externality and separateness are simply perceptual errors.

The Universal Principle of Harmony, Order and Balance
The universe is a model of supreme order, the perfection of
which is beyond the ability of the mortal mind to arrange,
imagine or describe, although this attempt is made by
many. The Earth revolves regularly on its axis, receiving the
sun's rays only on the surface facing the sun at each
moment, thus creating light and darkness, day and night.

With exquisite symmetry, each of the planets in the
solar system follows its own course around the sun.
Similarly, the negatively charged electrons orbit the positively charged nucleus of each atom.

Harmony is the subtle yet inviolable power of the
universe, whereas force and violence are aberrations. This
is fundamental universal law. Every positive manifestation
in the universe comes forth as the result of the creative,
harmonized union of yin and yang energies and each
manifestation has its own unique energy arrangement and
pattern of movement. Following the inherent order of the
universe results in harmony and balance; opposing the
cosmic principle of natural order creates destruction.

When artificial means are used, to split atoms for
example, the natural order of the atom is violated and
massive devastation as nuclear explosion is the result.
Whenever humankind creates radical change by violating
the laws of nature, the end result is destruction. There are
times when nature herself creates radical change, and,
although there may be destruction and a taking away of the
old, there is also creation of new life. However, if artificial
deviation from the state of universal order occurs, the
principles of cosmic law immediately go into effect to rectify
and balance the deviation, because disorder is against the
true nature of the universe and therefore cannot last.

Everything created and everything as yet uncreated
comes forth from the same Subtle Origin. And because
everything in the universe shares the same original source,
all of the parts of the universe share the same true nature
as the whole, from the most minute atomic particle to the
most vast and magnificent star. The true nature of the

universe and thus that of every human being is creative, productive, progressive, orderly and harmonious. Aberrant thinking and behavior, that is, thinking and behavior which deviate from the natural universal moral order of harmony, balance and productivity, will absolutely evoke a negative response from the corresponding universal energies, as surely as a shadow follows its form.

Since all of our behavior is an extension of what is held in the mind, it is necessary to set the mind in right order so that it contains only positive energy to be rightly manifested in our lives. Carefully choose your thoughts, emotional reactions and words; weed out those negative in nature because they will attract the negative energies of the same frequency which will manifest in your life as negative experience and harmful results. By engaging in constructive, creative activities which are beneficial not only to yourself but to others as well, you increase the interaction of the internal and external positive energies and thereby attract the response of the corresponding energies of the universe.

Whether or not one has set high spiritual goals for oneself, it is essential to thoroughly understand the principle of response and attraction of energy and to use it scrupulously because the success of both worldly life and spiritual growth depends upon such understanding. If it is one's spiritual goal to connect one's energy with that of the highest realms of the universe, the foundation upon which one's self-cultivation must be built is the principle of energy response. The seeker of the deeper reality of life must have a strong, virtuous character and a sense of moral responsibility as a prerequisite to learning the subtle universal truths. To reform a selfish, ruthless person who goes against the universal laws of natural physics is to destroy a demon; to instruct an individual in a strong sense of moral responsibility and obedience to the subtle laws of life is to instruct him in becoming a divine being.

Universal law is absolute and impartial. It can be evaded by no one. The cosmic laws of energy are just as

binding on sages as they are on ordinary individuals. Were
they something one could adhere to today and escape
tomorrow, they would be of no more consequence than our
artificial man-made laws. The purpose of learning universal
law is to gain self-mastery and peace. We lack tranquility in
our lives because we have strayed from our true nature and
lost our knowledge of universal law, which is not outside us
but within. After all, individuals are the embodiment of
universal law itself, manifesting as human beings.

If then we follow our true inner nature, we will be
following universal law. The problems in our lives are
generally not caused by seriously immoral behavior, but
rather by our unconscious violation of the correct order of
energy. Many people may be interested in spiritual disci-
plines or traditions, but without understanding the laws of
energy, one will still manifest disharmony in one's life
despite the acquisition of spiritual knowledge and
techniques.

Despite the fact that transgressions against natural law
may sometimes appear to go unnoticed by the universe, the
fruits of the violations must inevitably be harvested. This
cosmic law is just as impartial in the mental realm as is the
law of gravity in the physical realm, and its influence is just
as inescapable.

The Yin and Yang Principle in Behavior
In order to achieve harmony in one's behavior it is necessary
to balance the yin and yang, to integrate the yin and yang
as one unit again. For instance, it is not enough to develop
wisdom and understanding. In spiritual learning, wisdom
and understanding are considered yin qualities. To achieve
only these without cultivating the yang energy to realize
these qualities is to have one-sided development. Anything
one-sided is incomplete.

The integral approach to personality development
classifies some virtues as yin and some as yang. These
need to be balanced. Patience is a good virtue to develop,
and it is a yin or passive virtue. Progressiveness, a yang or

active virtue, is also a desirable virtue to cultivate. Patience and progressiveness must stand in balance within one's personality. When yin and yang are combined, we have complete virtue. Incomplete virtue can cause disaster. Take kindness as an example. Without the application of intelligence, kindness, itself a cardinal virtue, would be only blind kindness which can do much damage. In the physical realm, nature demonstrates blind kindness by supporting poison ivy as well as beneficial plants. We must remember that a human being is not merely a manifestation of the physical aspect of the universe. He is rather a complete model of the universe, demonstrating the physical as well as mental and spiritual aspects of existence. Thus one must not only be kind, but intelligent as well, and vice versa.

The principle of yin and yang is also demonstrated in the realm of the emotions. For example, sentiment is a yin type of emotion, while joy is a yang type; worry is yin, while anger is yang. All emotional elements should find moderate expression on appropriate occasions or one will destroy the normal balance of one's feelings.

An important point to remember is that the sage does not employ a strict dogmatism in the question of proper behavior. He rather takes a more empirically provable stance. By intelligently applying the principles of yin and yang, and by observing the efficacy of these truths, one is provided with a scientific tool for accomplishing specific desired results. With such a tool, one may achieve harmony and balance in all aspects of one's life.

Chapter 3

The Human Body and Universal Law

The study of the principles of the Integral Way invariably leads one to inquire into the art of acupuncture. As we come to understand that the spiritual process is one of harmonizing and refining one's physical, mental and spiritual energy, it becomes important to know the mechanics of the energy system and its operation in the human body. One also needs to clearly understand that this knowledge of the oneness of the human body, mind and spirit was not obtained through dissecting the body and observing its anatomy as is the practice in western medical research. It may seem amazing, but the ancient spiritually achieved ones used their mental ability of clear and unimpeded vision and recognition to compile the knowledge of the energy circulation in the channel system of the human body. Even if one is not interested in spiritual evolution, it is valuable to understand the principles of energy within the body in order to maintain one's equilibrium and health, both physically and mentally.

Acupuncture, a facet of the integral healing system, is a precise science dealing with the processing, storage, distribution and functioning of vital energy within the human organism, and the relationship of this energy to the cosmos. Acupuncture affects the circulation of energy within the human being on an extremely subtle level. The ancient achieved ones discovered that there is a subtle energy manifestation circulating throughout the organs and flesh which ultimately permeates every tissue and cell of the body. The name given to this energy is chi, which has been translated as "vital energy" or "life force." Human beings are the embodiment of all the energies of the universe, including the energies of the sun, moon and stars as well as the various energies of the Earth.

For thousands of years, the spiritually developed ones have had a clear understanding of the inseparability and dynamic interplay of man and nature. The energies embodied by an individual and the energies of the cosmos follow the same natural laws. Thus, the principles of yin and yang and the five phases of energy evolution operate within the human body, just as they do in the vast body of the cosmos, and their systematic symbolisms are likewise applied to the metaphysical medicine developed in ancient China.

The five phases of energy evolution have their corresponding internal organs: wood corresponds with the liver and gallbladder; fire corresponds with the heart, small intestine, pericardium and triple warmer; earth corresponds with the spleen/pancreas and the stomach; metal corresponds with the lungs and large intestine; water corresponds with the kidneys and bladder. The climatic conditions of the four seasons, including wind, rain, lightning, thunder and frost, also have their corresponding manifestations within the body. All of these transformations of bipolar energy interact within a human being, producing the life manifestations known as body, mind and spirit in their various expressions of personality.

The Channels
The energies of the human organism have clearly distinct and established pathways, definite directions of flow, characteristic behavior, etc., quite as definite as any other circulation within the body, such as the circulation of blood and lymph through their respective systems. The ancient achieved ones observed that illness often produced painful areas upon the skin and that the pain would disappear when a cure was effected. They also noticed that stimulation or sedation of various points on the body produced an effect upon the functioning of internal organs. Thus, a stimulation of a point below the knee might affect the face, and yet another point on the thumb would affect the lungs or throat.

After countless years of observation and experience in treatment and response, a systematic order of these sensitive points was formulated. These sensitive points were classified into twelve main groups and two minor groups. All the points of a specific group could be connected by a line which was considered the path the energy of the body followed as it circulated throughout the organism. The final results of these observations were correlated and refined over thousands of years. From the results, it was deduced that there were lines of transmission of energy which not only connected all of the organs of the body, but also connected the external to the internal.

The detection of these pathways of energy is analogous to finding an underground watercourse of springs sent up through "punctures" in the earth's crust. The sensitive points provide the positive data on which the theory is based; the pathways, on the other hand, are only the result of systematic speculations. These pathways which distribute the energies occur externally on the skin, and also pass deep inside the body through the organs. They were originally charted in prehistoric times. However, to this day, no conclusive physiological equivalent has been discovered. The ancient sages discovered that these lines were the pathways for cosmic energy and that they connected not only the organs to one another, but also the organs to the cosmos. The study of these internal and external communications and the interrelationships of organs constitutes the central objective of all integral healing.

Within the body there are three circulations of life force: the inner or core circulation which flows through and unites the internal organs; the peripheral or surface circulation, which is located in the subcutaneous tissue and the connecting circulation which joins the two. The vital energy circulating throughout the human organism is generated, transformed, stored and distributed by the internal organs.

The paths of energy circulation in and among the organs themselves cannot be acted upon directly. Although the inner circulation and the circulation linking the inner and peripheral are not directly accessible, they may be influenced through the surface points. The various control or key points on these channels are well established. These points at which life force can be effectively and predictably controlled are known as acupuncture points. They have been called acupuncture points because the chief traditional method of influence is by means of inserting and manipulating a needle.

Some of these points are used to control surface energy directly, some to influence indirectly the core energy, and some to influence the intermediate circulations which link the core and peripheral circulations or which constitute energy reserves. At these points, energy imbalances, deficiencies, excesses, blockages, and leaks can be restored to normal balance.

The sages divided all of the channels into classifications of yin and yang based upon the polarization of energy within the body. All of the yang channels connect with the organs involved in the intake and digestion of food, and with the excretive organs. All of the yin channels connect with the organs active in the transformation and storage of the energy obtained from food. Each channel carries the name of the organ it is primarily associated with. The twelve main channels are the channels of the energies of the organs, each of which may be classified in terms of yin and yang as well as through the five phases of energy evolution:

lungs	*yin polarity corresponding with metal*
large intestine	*yang polarity corresponding with metal*
stomach	*yang polarity corresponding with earth*
spleen	*yin polarity corresponding with earth*
heart	*yin polarity corresponding with fire*
small intestine	*yang polarity corresponding with fire*
bladder	*yang polarity corresponding with water*
kidney	*yin polarity corresponding with water*
pericardium	*yin polarity corresponding with fire*
triple warmer	*yang polarity corresponding with fire*
gall bladder	*yang polarity corresponding with wood*
liver	*yin polarity corresponding with wood*

THE DAILY ENERGY CYCLE OF THE CHANNELS

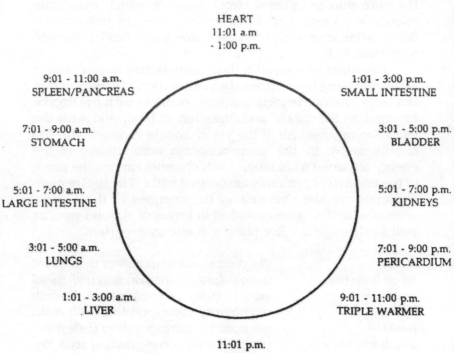

HEART
11:01 a.m
- 1:00 p.m.

9:01 - 11:00 a.m.
SPLEEN/PANCREAS

1:01 - 3:00 p.m.
SMALL INTESTINE

7:01 - 9:00 a.m.
STOMACH

3:01 - 5:00 p.m.
BLADDER

5:01 - 7:00 a.m.
LARGE INTESTINE

5:01 - 7:00 p.m.
KIDNEYS

3:01 - 5:00 a.m.
LUNGS

7:01 - 9:00 p.m.
PERICARDIUM

1:01 - 3:00 a.m.
LIVER

9:01 - 11:00 p.m.
TRIPLE WARMER

11:01 p.m.
- 1:00 a.m.
GALL BLADDER

(Figure 8)

The direction of the energy flow is highly important. In the human body, in general and under normal circumstances, yang energy flows upward and yin energy downward. The direction of the energy flow along the channels on the surface of the skin is easiest to picture when looking at the body flat, with the legs and arms fully extended in a straight line. Then all the yin channels flow toward on the front side of the body to concourse in the chest and all the yang channels move toward the back of the body. All of the channels are connected and polarized in such a manner that the circulation of energy throughout the body flows in a continuous and constant pattern.

There are eight extra channels. The two most important are the tu mo or governing vessel, "which controls all the yang channels and relates to the spiritual aspect of one's being, and the jen mo or "vessel of conception," which controls the yin channels and relates to metabolism.

The internal energy circulation is not limited to the jen mo and tu mo. All six yang channels, six yin channels and eight extra energy channels form the body's energy network. Details of the energy channels are given in acupuncture books.

Each channel experiences a waxing and waning of energy during the twenty-four hour cycle. The peak of this flow lasts two hours for each channel.

Three types of internal energy movement or internal exercise were created: the small orbit circulation, the big orbit circulation and the circulation of the eight extra energy channels. Only the small orbit circulation is done in sitting practice. The other two are done as standing and movement practices.

Integral Healing and Universal Law
The basis of all integral healing is the cosmic law of yin and yang. The continued existence or harmony of any individual, phenomenon or circumstance depends upon maintaining the appropriate equilibrium of yin and yang. The maintenance of this equilibrium is the function of the five phases

of energy evolution. If our internal and external environments remained constant, there would be no need for a regulating mechanism, but this is not the case. Life itself is not simply a series of static conditions. Rather, it is a constantly changing series of processes occurring as fluctuations between complementary polarities. Thus there must be a system of controls, not only to maintain the balance between these polarities within the organism, but also to regulate the exchange between the living system and its environment. This is the function of the five phases of energy evolution.

If the normal cycle of energy transformation is disturbed or violated, sickness and disease will appear. Then, instead of mutually assisting each other and controlling the proper balance, the five phases compete with and destroy each other. The system of the five phases of energy evolution describes the process of homeostasis within the body far more precisely and completely than any of the attempts made by its western counterparts. Homeostasis is defined as the automatic self-regulating system of controls that maintains the internal environment of living things and regulates the balance between the internal and the external.

All living things are homeostatic; otherwise they could not survive. The more complex the organism is, the more vital the process of homeostasis becomes. When homeostasis fails, the organism first suffers and then ultimately dies. The fundamental goal of integral healing is the maintenance of homeostasis through the application of the cosmic principles of yin and yang and the five phases of energy evolution.

The Organs - A General Overview
Before embarking on a discussion of the organ system according to integral healing, it is of utmost importance to recognize the vast differences between the western and the integral understanding regarding the functioning of the body.

Western anatomy is concerned with the human organism as a structure which may be taken apart like pieces of machinery to determine how the parts fit together and work. This approach implies that the form brings about the function. The ancient spiritual approach, on the other hand, deals with an individual life as an interrelationship of body, mind and spirit.

From this perspective it is recognized that in the natural development of human life, structure and form follow the function of life itself. In its specific discernment of the life functions, integral healing deals not with fixed, tangible entities but with what might best be described as twelve functional systems or energy spheres. It is these systems of energies in the body which enable a person to breathe, digest his food, move and think. The dynamic interplay of these energies is responsible for all the functions and expressions of the body, mind and spirit.

According to traditional integral medicine, the concept of an organ encompasses much more than a mere physical entity. When an organ is referred to in integral medicine, it is defined not by physical properties, but by its specific roles in the processing, storage and distribution of vital energy. Modern medicine deals with material structures and tissues which are able to perform certain functions. Integral medicine deals with the functions to which physical organs are attached.

When the term "organ" is used, it does not simply refer to an anatomical entity but rather to the manifestation of a functional sphere of energy which may or may not, as in the case of the triple warmer, include a physical counterpart. Therefore, statements regarding a certain organ can under no circumstances be made to agree completely with statements about the corresponding organ in western thought.

The organ spheres are further distinguished by particular qualities corresponding to phases of the cosmic cycles which determine the organ's special responsibilities for keeping the body in harmony with nature. Through understanding the operation of cycles of energy transformation, it is possible to relate the physiological activities within the human organism to their counterparts in nature. The very same transformations of energy which create the heavenly bodies, the Earth and the four seasons also create the corresponding organs within the human body.

Each organ is the functional representation within the body of a specific phase in the cycle of energy evolution. As such, each organ corresponds with all other manifestations of that particular phase which exist in the universe. Therefore, the definition of an organ is not limited to just the physical organ within the body. It includes all of the phenomena of the body, both internal and external, which are manifestations of the energy of the organ. It also includes all of its correspondences in the external universe, according to the five phases of energy evolution. For a more detailed account of the organs, refer to the Appendix at the back of this book.

Energy Manifestations within the Body

Chi

> *Change, both inception and transformation, rests on chi, and there is no being in the cosmos that does not originate from it. Thus chi envelops the cosmos from without and moves the cosmos from within. How else than by chi can the sun and moon, the planets and fixed stars shine; can thunder resound and rain, wind and clouds be formed; can all beings take rise, mature, bear fruit and withdraw in the course of the four seasons? Man's existence too depends upon this chi.* (Nei Ching)[3]

Chi is the vital universal energy which composes, permeates and moves everything that exists. Chi may be

-----

[3]The *Nei Ching* is known in English as *The Yellow Emperor's Internal Book.*

defined as the ultimate cause, and at the same time, as the ultimate effect. Chi is the ultimate essence of the universe as well as the law of all movement. When chi conglomerates, it is called matter. When chi is diffuse, it is called space. When chi animates form it is called life. When chi separates and withdraws from form, it is called death. When chi flows, there is health. When chi is blocked, there is sickness and disease. Chi embraces all things, circulates through and sustains them. The planets depend on it for their brightness, weather is formed by it, the seasons are caused by it. The *Nei Ching* says: "In Heaven there is chi and on Earth form. When the two interplay there is life."

So it is chi or vital energy which activates and maintains all life. Chi animates all the processes of the body: the digestion and assimilation of the food we eat, the inhalation and exhalation of air by the lungs, the circulation of the blood, the dissemination of fluids throughout the body, and finally the excretion of waste products of the metabolism. It is the chi of the various organs which enables the five senses to perform their functions:

> *One is able to smell only if the lung chi penetrates to the nose. One can distinguish the five colors only if the liver chi penetrates to the eyes. One can taste only if the heart chi penetrates to the tongue. One can know whether food is palatable only if the spleen chi penetrates to the mouth. The capabilities of the seven orifices depend upon the penetration of chi from the five solid organs."* (Su-Wen)

Although the unitary nature of chi never changes, this one bi-polar energy exhibits itself in many different forms and varieties. When referring to chi in general, chen chi is the healthy, physical vitality or physical essence and hsieh chi the vicious, unhealthy energy in the body. Yuan chi designates the subtle vitality of a human being in its entirety, and ching chi the reproductive energy and the essential physical energy. In the terminology of integral physiology, yeng chi signifies the liquid, visible energies, and wei chi the invisible energy of the body.

A new human being is conceived when the refined life essences, the ching chi of the father and mother, meet and fuse within the womb. This fusion produces the yuan chi - the subtle vital energy which is the foundation of the new human being's physical and mental structure. It can modify itself to cope with external demands but its essential nature cannot be changed. At death, it dissolves into its component parts, the physical aspect returning to the Earth and the subtle aspects returning to Heaven, the subtle realm of existence. The yuan chi is the primal energy of an individual. During pregnancy the yuan chi of the new individual relies solely upon the mother for its nourishment through the umbilical cord. After birth, the yuan chi is sustained by the activity of the organs. It functions to aid in the transformation of energy from food. Its residence in the body is the energy center located below the navel, the lower tan tien. The strength of an individual's yuan chi determines his life span. Its vigor cannot be increased but it can be dissipated through indulging in an excessive life-style. When the yuan chi is dissipated, one's natural life span is shortened. However, through practicing a quiet and simple way of life, it may gradually be restored.

Nourishment for the body is derived from two main sources, the food we eat and the air we breathe. Food, which contains the essences of the earth, is taken into the stomach where both the activity of the yuan chi and the heat produced by the middle burner distill its energies.[4] This essential energy distilled from food, the ku chi, is sent to the spleen for further refinement. The spleen then directs the ku chi to the lungs. Assisted by the heat produced in the upper burner, the essences of the earth from the food blend with the essences of Heaven from the air. This mixture is called chung chi. The chung chi is then acted

---

[4]Refer to "The Triple Warmer Sphere" in the appendix.

upon by the yuan chi in the lower tan tien, and transformed and further refined into chen chi or physical essence, a form of energy which is able to circulate throughout the body and meet the body's needs.

The *Ling-Shu*[5] states:

> *A person receives chi from food. The chi is extracted, stored and transmitted throughout the body by the activity of the six hollow and five solid organs. The clear components constitute the wei chi, the protective and defensive energy, and its murky components constitute the yeng chi, the nourishing and constructive energy. The yeng chi circulates within the blood vessels and ducts of the body, and the wei chi circulates outside of them.*

As elucidated above, the chen chi circulates throughout the body in two main forms. One is called the yeng chi, which carries the refined nourishment from food throughout the body and is the liquid energy of the body. The other form of energy which circulates throughout the body is called wei chi. Whereas the yeng chi circulates through the blood vessels, lymph ducts and the glandular system, the wei chi is diffused throughout the body. It is the invisible vitality which the ancient developed ones named specifically as chi. It manifests as a layer of warm atmosphere on the surface of the skin and circulates through the channel system and around all organs, muscles, and bones.

The function of the wei chi is to protect the body so that it can resist any invasion from external disease-causing influences. It also functions to warm the flesh, indirectly open and close the pores, maintain a healthy complexion, and protect the bones and joints. Any disease caused by an external factor indicates a malfunctioning of the wei chi. The nourishing yeng chi, because it is composed of rarefied

---

[5]The *Ling-Shu* is the second part of the *Yellow Emperor's Internal Book*, which contains a discussion of acupuncture.

substances and circulates with the blood and other watery energy of the body, is considered yin. The protecting wei chi is composed of fiery elements and classified as yang.

The yeng chi and wei chi both complement and mutually depend on each other. The yeng chi nourishes the body from the interior and the wei chi protects it from exterior influences. Nourishment cannot take place unless the body is sufficiently protected against disease; this protection cannot take place if the body is not nourished. It must be noted that although the concept of yeng chi as internal or nourishing and wei chi as external or protecting is traditionally stressed in this context, both actually function in the internal and external parts of the body.

The chi in the human body does not have a fixed form. Sometimes it appears in clear, invisible forms - for example as thermal energy in fevers; in vaporized form as in the moistening of the palms; or in the ionized state as during the practice of internal movement arts of energy circulation and especially of T'ai Chi movement and spiritual methods. Under other conditions the chi is "murky" or visible and appears in a liquid state as in sweating, diarrhea, a cold with a running nose, seminal and vaginal discharge, in tears, or when one's mouth is watering. The manifestation of chi in tangible or intangible form depends on the internal and external factors in one's life, on one's emotional energy, on the climate and so forth. If the chi is strong, it is ionized; if it is weak, it is liquefied.

The organs use the chi which circulates to them to maintain the life sustaining activities of the body. Any surplus energy is directed to the kidney sphere where it is transformed into ching chi, the essential physical energy and reproductive energy of the body, and where it is stored. The kidney sphere acts as a reservoir of refined energy which may be tapped by the organs whenever need arises. Sickness, traumatic injury, stress, indulgence in stimulants and excessive sexual activity result in a depletion of the ching chi. When ching chi is insufficient, the activities of both yeng chi and wei chi are greatly decreased, leaving the body inadequately nourished and vulnerable to disease. This ultimately weakens one's vitality.

The storage and consumption of ching chi take place normally throughout the year. However, the function of storing and retaining ching chi is especially active during autumn and winter. If sufficient ching chi is preserved during the winter, the diseases of spring weather will be repelled. Whenever life essence is required by the body, the kidneys release it so that it can circulate throughout the organs during times of stress. Thus, if the body is attacked by illness or becomes over-exhausted, the reserve of ching chi is consumed. If the supply of ching chi is abundant, the body's resistance to disease is maintained. As the reproductive energy, the ching chi is responsible for the production of the sperm and ova and determines the hereditary constitution of one's offspring. It is the fusion of the ching chi of both parents with the spirit of the new individual that produces the yuan chi and the fetus of a new life. If the ching chi becomes damaged, it will reflect in the other manifestations of the kidney sphere. For example, the bones and teeth may become soft and start to decay. This is especially noticeable in the case of a pregnant woman. Pregnancy takes a tremendous toll on the ching chi of the expectant mother unless it is replenished through diet and a natural life-style.

The ching chi matures in girls at the age of fourteen, after two periods of seven years, and in boys at the age of sixteen, after two eight-year periods. Likewise, menopause occurs in women after seven seven-year periods, while the equivalent happens in men after eight eight-year periods. The exact time span during which an individual is able to reproduce varies somewhat, of course, for each human being.

The ancient achieved ones discovered that chi is the definite and crucial indicator of the existence of life. Chi does not exist in a dead body. For an organism to have vital functions in the materialized sphere, it must contain yeng chi and wei chi. Integral medicine treats and takes into consideration all the integral vital functions of a human being at the same time: physical energy, emotional energy, mental energy, will power and spiritual energy. All the manifold functions of human life are merely different expressions of chi. Without the basic understanding of the function of chi, any medical treatment at best, is incomplete.

Blood

> The middle warmer receives chi, extracts the liquid
> and turns it red. This is called blood. (Ling-Shu).

The refined energy from food, known as ku chi, is not the only product derived from the transformation of the energy of food. The juices of the food are utilized for the formation and nourishment of the blood. Blood is produced and stored in the middle warmer, essentially the stomach, spleen and liver, from which it is distributed throughout the body in accordance with demand. Although blood and other liquids of the body are definite substances, they cannot be regarded as containing their own specific energy in the same manner as do the organs or tissues. This is because the blood itself must nourish the body and, therefore, its volume and composition change constantly. To meet this unstable situation, new blood must be constantly introduced in the same way that the yeng chi and wei chi must be replenished continuously. Blood therefore has more the properties of energy than of matter.

Yeng chi and blood are concerned with circulation and nourishment, and when these function normally the body is strong and all its mechanisms are working in unison. When the circulation of yeng chi and blood is blocked, disease occurs. Only if the vessels are so regulated that there is an uninterrupted circulation of blood can the skin, flesh, muscles, bones and joints of the body be strong, vigorous and supple. Thus, the reason the eyes can see, the feet walk, the hands grasp and the skin sweat is that they are all irrigated with blood. Chi controls the movement of the blood. Chi is the "general" of the blood; if chi moves, the blood also moves. Along the channels and blood vessels, the blood and the yeng chi travel together.

> *If chi and blood are not evenly balanced, then yin and yang will oppose each other; yeng chi will rebel against wei chi, blood against yeng chi, and blood and chi will be separated, one being full and the other empty.* (Ling-Shu)

Shen

Shen (which is also sometimes written sen) may be defined as the directing energy that determines and upholds the specific character of an individual. It is the energy responsible for the organization of an living individual. Shen represents a concept of "straight extension" which cannot be perceived directly. Shen may manifest itself, and thus be perceived, only to the degree that it meets with yin energy of complementary quality. Chi is the energy which constitutes an individual. What determines, produces and maintains the configuration of an individual's energy is shen. In the West, you often use the word "soul" to describe shen. However, in a life being, shen is the god which governs the life, and the soul is the sense of the individual. Thus, shen and soul are two different things. Shen is active in every phenomenon and on every evolving level as the influence that determines and maintains the configuration of an individual being or thing.

Shen is nourished by the essences distilled from air, food and water. It is the guiding spirit which directs the activities of the chi. Shen may be observed as four specific active groups in the body.

One active group called Po associates with the physical aspect, which is expressed in and especially works with the functioning of the lungs. The function of Po is to direct the physical energies - the yeng chi, wei chi, chen chi and yuan chi.

Another guiding spirit is Hun, the subtle aspect, which is expressed in the functioning of the liver sphere. The Hun represents the forces within a person which actively fashion the personality and direct the thinking faculties, both conscious and unconscious. The Po is considered yin and the Hun yang. One of the ancient spiritual classics defines the Po as the spirit (ling) that is attached to the form of things, while the shen that is attached to the chi of things is Hun.

The "I" (pronounced ee) is the conscious energy which is expressed through the functioning of the spleen sphere. This energy directs the processes of memory.

The chih or will power directs the processes of volition and is expressed through the functioning of the kidney sphere.

All of these functions are determined and controlled by the shen which resides in the heart sphere. Seeing, hearing, speaking, the consciousness and activity of the mind, and the movement of the body are all manifestations of shen. If the spirit is unable to function properly, actual disease will result. If the spirit is weak, the eyes are dull, the individual has no vitality and, in extreme cases, may talk nonsense and engage in insane actions.

Chapter 4

The Art of Preserving Health

The sages of ancient times emphasized not the treatment of disease, but rather the prevention of its occurrence. To administer medicines to diseases which have already developed and to suppress revolts which have already begun is comparable to the behavior of one who begins to dig a well after he has become thirsty and of one who begins to forge his weapons after he has already engaged in battle. Would these actions not be too late? (Su-Wen)

The essential art of integral medicine is the foreseeing and preventing of disease rather than the treatment of illness after it has manifested as painful or distressing physical and mental symptoms. As the emphasis of modern medicine is the restoration of health in those who are already sick, it gives little attention to maintaining the good health of someone who is well. With the integral system, however, it is possible to discover energy imbalances long before they are seen as an overt disease. It is also possible to adjust one's life so as to be in harmony with natural law in order to avoid creating such imbalances.

From the point of view of modern medicine, health is merely the absence of disease. Yet by taking a preventive route, one may elevate one's general state of health to a level at which one may consistently enjoy a positive feeling of well-being with an abundance of physical and mental energy. Frequently, people may not actually feel ill but suffer from slight fatigue and other minor symptoms, decreasing their zest for life. By correcting these minor imbalances through the use of diet, exercise, and a general alteration of one's life regimen and mental habits, or through the use of therapies such as acupuncture, herbs, and other healing arts, one not only eliminates the problems, but in addition is spared the consequences of developing diseases later on.

According to integral medical theory, the causes of disease are primarily either external or internal. External causes are comprised mainly of climatic energy manifestations which may attack the organism from without. These climatic manifestations are referred to in the ancient classics as "vicious winds," and each is present during a particular season: spring is the season for wind, summer for heat and fire, Indian summer for dampness, fall for dryness, winter for coldness. Each climatic energy has an affinity for one of the five viscera which is particularly vulnerable to disease during that season according to the five phases of energy evolution.

If the organ is attacked by a "vicious wind" and the correct inner/outer balance is not restored quickly, the threatening energy will penetrate the organ and remain dormant until the next or following season. Therefore, fall dryness attacks the lungs and produces coughing in the fall and winter; winter cold attacks the kidneys and the general vitality and causes general weakness and fevers in the winter and spring; in the spring, wind attacks the liver and produces intermittent fevers and headaches in the spring and summer; the wetness of Indian summer attacks the spleen, and malaria type diseases and rheumatism result in the fall and winter. It is a wise practice to pay special attention to the season's organ during the times of change in weather because the root of a disease often lies here.

Although the types of "vicious winds" mentioned are prevalent in specific seasons, they exist in all seasons and comprise only the general climatic causes of disease. There are also other specific climatic influences. Blood pressure changes, for example, are unusual in cold weather, which causes the pores to close. Yet in hot weather an excessive amount of blood will rise to the head and sometimes this results in nostril or gum bleeding, or even in a "summer" stroke.

Internal causes consist primarily of excessive indulgence in a particular emotion. This weakens first the organ sphere whose energy is responsible for generating the emotion, and then in turn causes imbalance and disorder in the cyclic interrelationship of all the other organ spheres.

Other miscellaneous internal causes would be faulty diet, excessive fatigue, poisons, traumatic injuries, animal and insect borne diseases (parasitic), hereditary factors, mechanical or radiation damage, and epidemics. Any disturbance of the natural balance of the body, if allowed to continue, will create a state of ill health, ultimately shortening the individual's natural life span.

The *Ling-Shu* says: "If the energies are circulating correctly, no evil can attack successfully." The classics also state that "wind, rain, cold and heat, if not stealthy, cannot hurt." Climatic influences are "stealthy" only when one is not aware of them, pays no attention to them, and takes no preventative measures. Nevertheless, the body automatically and on its own will react to climatic influences and changes by gathering the chi within, and is able to protect itself from and resist the external influences to a certain degree. When one is cautious, then "even if the body is weak, strong winds and heavy rain cannot affect it. For disease to occur, there must be both, a stealthy evil and a weakened body." From this we can see that two conditions must prevail in order for illness to manifest: a disease-causing influence, and a receptive host - a body which is unprotected and weak enough to allow the influence to damage it.

There are four aspects to preserving good health according to the *Nei Ching*, the classic book on healing and health, which was compiled thousands of years ago by the famous Yellow Emperor. The four aspects are: nurturing the mind, engaging in proper physical exercise, maintaining an adequate, balanced diet, and adapting to the ever-changing environmental conditions. The aim of all of these approaches is the same, and that is to keep the individual in harmony with the natural law of the universe.

Emotions

> *In order to avoid the attacks of abnormal seasonal*
> *energies one must pay attention to nurture the spirit*
> *(mind) so that one feels at peace emotionally. When*
> *one is unemotional and carefree, the body's energy*
> *will be abundant and the mind well-guarded inside.*
> *How then can disease arise? Thus, when one's*
> *emotions are tranquil, one has few desires, one's heart*
> *is calm and not fearful One's body works but one is*
> *not fatigued. (Su-Wen)*

According to the integral medical system, the emotions
are classified into five predominant states: joy, reminiscence, sadness, fear and anger. These states correspond to
the five evolving phases of fire, earth, metal, water and
wood, respectively. It is interesting to note that love (jen) is
not considered an emotion but rather an activity of the
spirit. The five emotions are generated by the activities of
the five viscera when these are stimulated by external
change. Thus, the emotions are a manifestation of the
energy of the organ spheres and may be thought of as the
motivating energy of the body. The continual shift of
emotional states is a natural phenomenon initiated by the
automatic response of the visceral energy to changes in the
environment.

However, an emphasis on one particular emotion will
disrupt the natural cycles of energy transformation and
circulation within the body and throw an unbearable stress
upon the overstimulated organ. If continued to excess, this
stress from imbalance will cause pathological strain on the
organism, and disease will result. When one emotion is
expressed consistently, its parent organ first becomes
hypertense and then breaks down into pathological disorder.

By utilizing the creative and checking (destructive or
competitive) cycles of the five phases of energy evolution,
one may achieve emotional balance and harmony. Relating
this principle to diet, one may emphasize or decrease the
five specific flavors of one's food so as to enhance or control

the emotion corresponding to that particular element. For example, grief or sadness can be controlled by decreasing hot food and eating more bitter food, as well as by listening to the musical tone of the corresponding checking element. On the other hand, an excessive intake of salt will damage the kidneys and thus create fear.

Another application of this theory is the direct treatment of the energy spheres of the organs which generate the emotions. The *Nei Ching* says: "The liver stores blood. An excess of blood in the liver will cause anger and a deficiency will cause fear. If the liver holds back the blood it will cause madness." The *Su-Wen* further elucidates: "When energy and blood rise to the head a person is easily angered. Blood in excess will turn to anger. However, excessive anger exhausts the blood."

This refers especially to the nervous system, which is a manifestation of the energy of the liver sphere. When the cerebral nerves become congested with energy or deficient in energy, one's emotional states are greatly altered. From this we can see how closely related one's mental states are with the phenomena occurring in the body as the circulation of blood and energy. Thus, not only do the emotions influence one's physical body; emotional changes also affect one's spirit or consciousness in various ways.

Anger, the energy of the liver, rises upwards so that consciousness is strong in the head and shoulders. The nervous system, which corresponds with wood, extends the energy of the liver sphere and develops like a tree. The rising motion of the liver's energy can be evidenced by the fact that, when a person becomes angered, the blood will suddenly rush to the head and the face will become red.

Joy, the energy of the heart, suspends consciousness in the point of inhalation, and this suspension is a slowing down process which is concentrated in the upper warmer. If the expression of happiness is indulged in excessively, the energy of the heart becomes exhausted, affecting the functions of all the other spheres as well.

Grief or sadness is the energy of the lungs. Sadness disperses consciousness and leaves the body weak. The action of sadness causes one's energy to disintegrate and leak out of the body.

Fear, the energy of the kidneys, descends to the bowels and the lower extremities. This can be illustrated by the tendency of people in extreme fear to involuntarily move their bowels and become incontinent.

Shock is connected with the heart and means that consciousness is disturbed. In clinical practice, the beginning of an illness can often be traced back to a time of intense shock which weakened the system.

Reminiscence, the energy of the spleen, concentrates consciousness within the brain. This can be illustrated by the fact that when one continually ponders problems, the most frequent symptom experienced is insomnia. In this case, the energy stays in the brain at night instead of following its normal course of descending to the lower part of the body, which allows one to sleep peacefully.

Worry, another type of energy of the lungs, coagulates consciousness so that the body becomes paralyzed. When energy coagulates from worry, one becomes unable to do even the smallest tasks. Because the lungs are not moving freely, the person becomes prone to respiratory problems.

While emotions may be thought of as the motivating energy of the body, it is the spirit or shen which is the coordinator and overseer of the energies of the emotions. It is also the spirit which is ultimately weakened and damaged by emotional imbalance and excess. Because spirit or shen has such intimate connections with the emotions, any emotional stress will also affect the heart, the dwelling place of the shen. Because the heart sphere is the master of all the other spheres, when the heart is calm, the energy flows smoothly throughout all the other spheres and the energy of the body is in harmony.

Exercise

In order for a person to be well physically, mentally and spiritually, it is essential that his or her internal energies flow in an unimpeded and harmonious manner. What does this mean? Under ideal conditions, a person's internal energies orbit throughout his or her being in much the same way as the planets and other heavenly bodies orbit as they course through the vast body of the cosmos. In both cases, the orbits are determined by universal natural laws.

When stress is encountered by an individual during the course of daily life, the subconscious mind will direct extra energy to certain areas of the body to handle the stress. Over the course of time, the body becomes habituated to energizing certain areas and neglecting others, while the normal course of energy circulation is becoming distorted and unbalanced. In this case, the orbits no longer follow natural law. It is this distortion and deviation from the Way of the universe which results in personal disharmony, manifesting as physical disease, mental aberration or disastrous events in one's life.

The ancient spiritually achieved ones developed a system of physical movements which are based on the natural motion of the heavenly bodies. By moving the body in this fashion, one guides the internal energies to flow according to the same natural laws which keep the planets on course and the galaxies propelling through space in harmony. By practicing these energy-guiding exercises, one may unblock and relieve energy congestion in certain parts of the body and gradually eliminate the stress that has accumulated over the course of time. One may also redirect the flow of vitality so that every muscle, nerve and organ is nourished and tonified. For further information about exercises of the Integral Way, please refer to Chapter 5 and 6 on gentle T'ai Chi movement and natural movement of the Integral Way.

Diet

The principle of the five phases of energy evolution is the essential principle related to diet. The ancient developed ones classify foods as having five basic flavors: sour, bitter, sweet, hot (pungent) and salty, which correspond with the five viscera according to the law of the five elements. The *Ling-Shu* says: "Each of the five tastes moves to what it likes. If the taste of the nourishment is sour, it moves first to the liver; if bitter it moves first to the heart; if sweet, it moves first to the spleen; if hot (pungent) it moves first to the lungs; if salty it moves first to the kidneys."

The normal functioning of the energy sphere of the heart requires bitter and cooling-natured foods. Yet flavors which in moderate doses are beneficial to an organ, are injurious when taken in excess. Thus, an excess of bitter foods is detrimental to the normal functioning of the heart. However, one should not try to drain off excessive energy by eating too much of the corresponding bitter flavor, because this would tend to impair the ability of the heart to contract normally. Instead, one would use the sweet flavor for this purpose because it would help the circulation of the blood. However, a sugar imbalance will create problems too.

The normal functioning of the liver energy sphere requires sour food, yet an excess of sour foods drains off the energy of the liver and tends to exhaust it.

Sweet flavors are used to replenish the energy of the spleen. However, in the case of the spleen, the sweet flavor is not used to drain off excess energy because this flavor has a comforting, warming and tonifying effect. Instead, the bitter flavor is used to drain off excess energy of the spleen.

The lungs require pungent or hot foods for their normal functioning. An excess of energy in the lungs is drained off by large doses of its corresponding hot or pungent flavor, and a deficiency is replenished by the sour flavor.

The kidneys require a moderate amount of salty flavored foods to maintain their normal functioning. An excess of energy in the kidneys is drained off by its corresponding salty flavor, whereas its energy is replenished by the complementary bitter flavor.

Health is best maintained when a diet includes a balance of all five flavors. Foods which can cause imbalance and disease are: fats in excess quantity, cold and raw foods, large amounts of liquids, too much salty or sweet foods, and very dry or excessively bitter foods. One should not eat food that is cold because this damages the yang energy in the stomach and intestines and may produce symptoms of stomach ache, vomiting and diarrhea. Hot, dry foods produce excessive heat within the body, which could cause dry feces and hemorrhoids. Large amounts of liquids can cause a "wet condition" in the body which might manifest as digestive problems. Naturally, if one consumes too little food, the body will be deprived of one of its main sources of energy.

Environment

Harmonizing oneself with the changes in one's personal environment and living according to natural law are essential aspects of maintaining good health. This means that one should engage in activities which are in harmony with the energies of the season and conduct every aspect of one's life accordingly. The *Su-Wen* elucidates:

> *The three months in spring is the time when all living things begins to germinate and grow. At this time, nature is filled with a lively atmosphere and all things are alive. Go to bed when night comes and get up early. Wear your hair and garments loose and take a walk in your courtyard. Your mental and conscious activities can also be like the weather of spring - active and live (generation but not persecution, give but not take, encouragement but not chastisement). This then responds to the weather of spring and follows the principles of nurturing the energy of birth. If one goes against this principle, one would damage the liver energy (nervous system), and when summer comes*

'cold' types of disease will occur, and one's adaptability to the energy of summer will be weakened.

The three months of summer is the time when all the energy from the sky downpours and the energy from the earth uprises. From this interaction of sky and earth energies, all plants grow. They bear flowers and fruit. Go to bed later at night and get up early, not loathing the sunlight. Do not get angry easily and maintain a lively and pleasant spirit, calm and peaceful mind, so that one's shen is full, like all things in nature. Shen grows beautiful and strong. Do not block the pores of the skin so that you perspire freely, evaporating not only your sweat, but also your emotions and desires. In other words, all things should follow the principle of going outward; this is the way of nurturing growth in summer. If one goes against this rule, one damages the heart energy, and when fall comes malarial fevers will easily arise, so that one will not be able to cope with the harvesting energy of fall.

The three months of autumn is the time when all things are ripe and ready for harvest. The weather of this season is cool and plants look solitary. Go to bed earlier during this season and get up in the morning at daylight. Keep the emotions calm and peaceful. It is only by conserving one's spirit and keeping calm that one can cope with the solitary weather of fall. And it is also by this that one's lung energy can be purified. This is the way to nurture one's energy in the fall. If one goes against this rule, the lung energy will be damaged, so that when winter comes the system cannot digest food properly, as is shown in the bowel excretions. Going against this rule also weakens one's adaptability to cope with the storage of winter energy.

The three months of winter is the time when all living things should hide and be conserved. At this time water is turned into ice and the ground is cracked *by coldness. Nature shows an overall condition of hidden yang energy. Go to bed early and get up only when the sun is in the sky. One's emotions should not be allowed to be too explicit, as when one is truly contented. Avoid coldness but linger around warmth. Do not allow one's skin to perspire, avoiding any escape of yang energy with the sweat. This then is the adaptation to the weather of winter and is the way to nurture storage. If one goes against this rule, weakness and coldness in the extremities will occur when spring comes and one's adaptability to the growth energy of spring will be weakened.*

In conclusion, the most important principle for achieving and maintaining good health is the principle of moderation in all things.

Malicious winds frequently come and heavy rains frequently arise if the four seasons of Heaven and Earth do not maintain harmony with each other. They lose the Way. Thus they extinguish themselves and cease to exist. Only the sage follows the Way. Therefore, he does not have serious diseases. If all things do not lose the Way, their life energy is not exhausted. (Su-Wen)

Regulate daily life so that there is a balance between rest and activity, and so that one activity is not engaged in to the exclusion of others.

Any excessive activity in daily life will damage one's health. Prolonged looking at objects will damage blood, prolonged sleeping will damage energy, prolonged sitting will damage muscles, prolonged standing will damage bones, prolonged walking will damage tendons. These conditions are known as damages of the five toils. (Su-Wen)

Guidelines for Health

The traditional spiritual teachings include simple and general guidelines for health which were collected by an anonymous author who lived before the Ming dynasty, using the pen name "The Hermit of the Western Mountain." These writings deal with the protection and cultivation of a human's energy. If a person does not value life and is unwilling to cultivate the energy he or she embodies, it will be impossible to transcend the painful problems and suffering created by the mind. It is futile to search for many kinds of medicine in hopes of prolonging one's physical life to an extraordinary age. Yet regulating the habits of one's ordinary daily life - such as exercise, the quality of one's thoughts and desires, the expression of emotions, the intake of food and drink - can yield tremendous rewards. If one can become free of excessiveness, one can find peace and happiness.

The basic advice concerning the diet is to eat and drink with discrimination and when it is appropriate; that is, only when one is really hungry or thirsty. It is best to eat small amounts several times a day. Overeating will damage one's energy and health. Certain foods are unwholesome and to be avoided altogether. These are: cold, sticky or hard foods; meat from sick animals or those who died a natural death; and any foods which are difficult to digest. Too many grain products will obstruct the energy flow in the body. Excessive amounts of any one of the five different flavors - salty, sweet, sour, bitter and hot (pungent) - will damage the energy of the five viscera. Excessive salt intake, for example, causes kidney disorders. Excessive sugar consumption leads to high blood pressure and other diseases related to the condition or circulation of the blood, such as inflamed gums or headaches from blood congested in the head. Raw fish and meat may upset the digestive system, as may spicy or greasy foods. Foods which have been preserved for a long time, such as pickled foods, are to be avoided completely by the elderly and eaten only in small quantities by the young.

Baked or roasted foods need to cool off somewhat because the heat will damage the gums and teeth.

In general, it is good to abstain from consuming anything which is very hot or very cold. Cold drinks in hot weather may induce a disorder of the stomach energy and possibly cause diarrhea. If one drinks wine, choose good quality wine and drink it at room temperature and in moderation. Getting drunk damages the mind and brain, and the thirst arising out of alcohol consumption leads to a high intake of other liquids and the retention of fluids in the body. In the summer, alcohol should be avoided completely. Drinking strong tea overstimulates the brain and causes the body to become cold and less energetic. One or two cups of tea after meals, however, are permissible because they aid in digestion and dissolve the grease from foods. When one is hungry, strong tea is detrimental, but when one has overindulged in alcohol it assists in becoming detoxicated.

If dinner is eaten late in the evening, the unutilized food will produce an energy stagnation in the stomach. Retiring when one is drunk is equally harmful. On the other hand, listening to peaceful and graceful music or taking a short walk will aid the digestion. One may also massage the stomach lightly with both palms and thereafter the kidney area. Then raise one's hands above the head and exhale three to five times through the mouth in order to eliminate the heat and toxins from the food. This practice is called "generating water and earth."

Practical teachings recommend some techniques and habits which are beneficial for one's energy. It is important to keep the body warm and to use warm water for bathing and brushing one's teeth. A cold bed or pillow can disturb one's energy. Combing one's hair frequently, rubbing one's face, biting one's teeth and swallowing one's saliva help to refine one's energy. The strengthening of one's internal organs and brightening of the face is accomplished by rubbing the backs of the thumbs together to produce heat; then gently stroking over the eyes fourteen times, over the sides of the nose thirty-six times, then with the palms fourteen times over the ears and fourteen times over the face. The best sleeping position for conserving one's energy is on the side and with the knees pulled up slightly. This is a protection from the intrusion of external energies which may cause nightmares. To sleep peacefully, turn off all lights and remain silent while lying down. When awakening, it is good to stretch thoroughly.

The different seasons of the year require certain precautions. The summer especially is a difficult season for taking good care of oneself. Sweating may cause no trouble in the summer, but in the winter, avoid it as much as possible because it creates a loss of energy in the body and weakens it. In autumn and winter, stay indoors until sunrise if possible. In spring and summer, it is time to rise when the rooster crows. Not earlier than the rooster crows or not earlier than sunrise in the cold winter when you still live a natural life. (A rooster usually crows during a three hour range before sunrise.) Also, do not rise later than sunrise. Another general precaution is not to walk in the mist, in the dark, or during thunderstorms.

The body needs to be protected from strong wind, particularly when sitting or lying down and after exercise or the consumption of alcohol, both of which open the pores and increase one's vulnerability to the wind. If a constant draft on the head goes unnoticed, for example, it may cause severe headaches.

The containment of one's physical and mental desires is of great importance. Physical and mental energies need to be balanced and in harmonious interplay with each other. To be idle physically and yet entertaining a busy mind is a waste of one's energy; working diligently and keeping one's mind at leisure is a healthy way of life. If one has strong mental energy and low vitality, be careful to engage only moderately in sexual activity.

Even in such matters as looking at objects, listening to sounds, and walking or sitting, excessiveness will be a reason for disorder. The body needs exercise to remain healthy and to be full of energy, but it can suffer from unreasonable physical demands. As a general but valuable guideline, adhere to the principle of moderation in all things. Approaching each situation with moderation will assure a balanced and harmonious life.

Ancient spiritual culture is rich in methods and regimens which promote health and longevity. "The Six Basic Soundless Sounds for Health" are an old and popular breathing technique which was practiced by people who lived to be over a hundred years of age. This technique is effective in both preventing and curing not only ailments of the organ spheres mentioned previously, but also of the manifestations and extensions of the energy of the organ spheres. Each of the six vibrations has a psychic influence on its corresponding organ sphere which prompts the expulsion of impurities from the sphere and its manifestations, and the gathering of fresh energy into each system.

During the yang period of the daily energy cycle, between midnight and midday and preferably very early in the morning, sit facing the east with your legs crossed. Close your eyes, clear your mind and concentrate your spirit. Gently inhale the fresh air, then vigorously exhale the expended air two or three times. Bite the teeth together thirty-six times, roll the tongue around until the mouth is full of saliva, rinse the mouth with the saliva a few times and then swallow it in three audible gulps, directing it with your mind to the lower tan tien, the psychic energy center below the navel.

Under the tongue there are two points which are connected with the glandular system. When you move your tongue up and down to stimulate the production of saliva until the mouth is full and then slowly swallow it, you will cause the response of all glandular secretions and concentrate all of your energy in the three psychic centers of the body - the three tan tien. This practice can also be performed lying down as long as your pillow is not too high.

Then pucker your lips and slightly and silently make the sound "Ho!" Close your mouth again to breathe in the fresh air through the nostrils to invigorate the heart. Your exhaling should be short and your inhaling long. Repeat this thirty-six times.

After that follow the same method and produce each of the other five sounds thirty-six times: "Hu" to invigorate the stomach and spleen; "Szz!" to invigorate the lungs; "Shu!" to invigorate the liver; "Shi!" to invigorate the gallbladder; and "Fu!" to invigorate the kidneys.

Each vibration must be made gently, subtly and inaudibly. If the sound is coarse and audible it will hurt the chi of the body. Generally, inhale through the nose and exhale through the mouth when practicing these vibrations. The principles is to exhale the old impure chi and to inhale the new chi. If each vibration is generated correctly it will be possible to feel its response in the corresponding organ. When the chi directly reaches the organs, they are revitalized and the health of one's entire being is enhanced.

The vibration "Ho" relates to the heart. The heart influences the blood supply to all the other organs and disorder of the heart will negatively affect the energy flow in the whole body. If one's heart experiences a shock and the spirit is disturbed, or if one is cold and feels the incessant need to talk to someone the vibration "Ho" should be used. It will balance the energy of the heart sphere and restore peace. The heart sphere is associated with the mental energy and its main representation in the head is the tongue. When the tongue is hot and dry, the vibration "Ho" is helpful.

If one's digestion is poor and the stomach feels bloated, apply the vibration "Hu," which is the vibration of the stomach and spleen energy. It is beneficial for any strong fever, cholera, stomach or side pain, or the feeling of heaviness in the stomach. The lips are connected with the spleen energy and therefore the vibration "Hu" benefits dry lips. Use the same vibration while inhaling and exhaling, and be sure to control the lips in order to avoid inhaling cold air through the mouth.

The sound "Szz" is the vibration of the lungs and will aid lung problems. If one's lung energy is weak, then one's breathing will be shallow and hard. If the lungs are dry, the throat too will become dry. If wind is held in the lungs, sweat will appear and one will fear the wind. Because the nose and the pores of the skin fulfill the same function as the lungs, the vibration "Szz" may help remedy skin problems or a cold with a stuffy nose. Again, it is important to keep the sound "Szz" inaudible.

The vibration corresponding with the liver is "Shu." The eyes will react sensitively to a disturbance of the liver energy through emotional tensions. Thus if the liver is congested with blood, the eyes will become congested and red. The liver is also associated with the nervous system, especially with the head area. Energy blockages in the nervous system will cause emotional and psychological problems. The vibration "Shu" will relieve distress of the nervous system, of the eyes and the liver itself. When practicing this vibration, open the eyes widely.

The sound "Shi" corresponds with the gallbladder. If the energy of the gallbladder is disordered, one may have a bitter taste in the mouth and vomit acidic liquid. If the gallbladder is weak, one may easily become frightened or cold. There may also be a tendency to feel dizzy and weak. For these symptoms, practice the vibration, "Shi." Then sit upright and meditate facing the North in order to gather the mystical chi from the North. This will help to replenish the chi lost in generating this vibration. Inhale the chi through the nose, bring it down into the mouth and swallow it in three gulps.

The vibration "Fu" corresponds with the kidneys. Imbalances of the kidney energy may cause one's hair to become dry, fingernails and toenails to wither, and the eyes to shed tears for no reason. The ears are the manifestations in the head area of kidney energy. Kidney energy disorders may include problems in those areas as well as coldness or pains at the waist, lower back or abdominal pain, and various sexual problems. All respond to the vibration "Fu." When making this vibration, blow the air gently through the mouth. If "vicious chi" descends from the lungs to the kidneys, it will cause much groaning, which can be alleviated by the sound "Fu." When one feels the lower part of the body become heavy, use a strong blowing out of the sound "Fu" in order to stimulate the energy flow.

The Six Basic Soundless Sounds for Health may be used for a general balancing of one's energy only.[6] Any serious disorder requires treatment with acupuncture, herbs, and related healing arts.

Each element in our ordinary, daily lives ushers in a powerful influence that eventually shapes our total well-being. The normal habits of each day have great value for the power they convey in the course of our lives on a grander scale. Diet, exercise, hours of sleeping and rising, emotions, desires, language, the very way we breathe - all these seemingly insignificant details weave together a pattern forming the rich tapestry of our health and vitality.

---

[6]For further information on the six healing sounds, see also *Ascend the Spiritual Mountain*, Chapter 14 (or the *Uncharted Voyage Toward the Subtle Light*, Chapter 48) and *The Power of Natural Healing*, Chapter 13.

Chapter 5

T'ai Chi Movement, Universal Law And the Law of Individual Being

Ancient achieved people deeply observed the operation of nature and developed a series of movements based on cosmology and patterned after the movement of the universe. T'ai Chi movement is one of the most popular of these systems. Based on the principle that the human body is a miniature universe, the system of gentle movement aims to guide an individual's energy through his or her microcosmic energy network in a manner which exactly follows cosmic law. By consistently harmonizing oneself with cosmic law in this way, physical health improves, the mind becomes clear, and the spirit becomes strong and tranquil.

It is the virtue or inherent quality of the universe to support all life. However, violation of universal law cuts one off from that support. T'ai Chi movement provides the means by which realignment with universal law may occur. In this way, one may enjoy the support of the universe in all aspects of life. Through the practice of T'ai Chi movement, the intellectual concept of the laws of nature is transformed into actual physical experience. By observing how one's own body and energy operate while performing T'ai Chi movement, one may discover experientially the law inherent in individual being. When one knows the law of individual being one knows the law of the universe.

The exploration of Tao as universal law through the practice of T'ai Chi movement begins with an understanding of the concepts of Taoist cosmology. However, it is only through experiencing the validity of universal law that its power to transform one's life can be realized.

Undivided Oneness - The Root of All Movement
The first principle of T'ai Chi movement is that undivided oneness is the root of all movement. From the perspective of cosmology, undivided oneness is the origin of every

manifestation in the universe. As the undivided oneness of the primal energy moves, it polarizes, creating yin and yang. The interactions and combinations of the polarities resulting from this movement bring forth the myriad manifestations. Thus, undivided oneness is the source of both the evolution and devolution of the multi-universe.

The T'ai Chi is the integration of yin and yang polarities. The polarization of the primal energy as it alternates between yin and yang is not a divisive or separating process. The polarizing movement is always integrated by the power of undivided oneness. If it were a division rather than an integrated movement, the multi-universe would inevitably come to an end. An illustration of undivided oneness might be the way a person uses each leg alternately in the process of walking. Each leg cooperates with the other and both are governed by the oneness of the person who is walking. The principle of undivided oneness applies in T'ai Chi movement as well as in the reality of daily life.

When we are born, our body, mind and spirit are perfectly harmonized and integrated. However, in the process of living in the world, the body, mind and spirit drift farther and farther apart until their ultimate disintegration, which is death. At death, the soul or yang polarity returns to the subtle realm and the body or yin polarity to the physical realm. A human being dies because he is no longer able to integrate the yin and yang vibrational polarities of his being. The shen, the energy responsible for the organization of the individual being, no longer functions to integrate and direct its energies, and the po (yin) and the hun (yang), the I (yin) and the chih (yang), cannot fulfill their respective functions.

The multi-universe is infinite because it continuously integrates its polarities through its exquisite pattern of movement. In the human body, T'ai Chi movement brings physical, emotional, mental and spiritual energies into alignment once again as undivided oneness. When a person achieves the integration of his own internal polarities through the practice of T'ai Chi movement, this in turn will cause the response of harmony and unification of all the apparent opposites which appear externally and internally in his life.

The term used to describe the undivided oneness, the source of all movement, is wu chi, the Infinite One or the Ultimate Oneness. You may say that T'ai Chi, the natural law, proceeds from wu chi. Yet wu chi is in T'ai Chi and T'ai Chi is contained in wu chi. There is no separation between the conditions of T'ai Chi and wu chi, just as there is no separation between yin and yang and undivided oneness.

Yin and Yang and the Principle of Symmetry

All movement may be explained in terms of yin and yang. For example, leftward movement is yang, rightward movement is yin. Upward movement is yang, downward movement is yin. Inhalation is yang, exhalation is yin, and so forth. The movements of T'ai Chi exercise are a continual sequence of yin and yang movements. If there is an upward movement, then there is a low movement to balance it. If there is a movement to the left, then there is a movement to the right to give it symmetry. Inhalation and exhalation are also coordinated with each movement so that yin and yang, which are sometimes also called the negative and positive vibrational polarities of the human energy system, are always balanced.

The Alternation of Stillness and Movement

Through their deep observation of the movement and development of the universe, the ancient developed people discovered the natural law that stillness and movement alternately follow each other. In the general sense, movement is yang and stillness is yin. Many spiritual traditions emphasize quiet sitting meditation. Yet quiet sitting alone tends to wither one's vitality because it causes one's energy to stagnate. If one practices quiet sitting exclusively, one hastens the degeneration of one's life, rather than furthering one's spiritual evolution.

In the Integral Way, it is understood that in order to derive full benefit from quiet sitting meditation, it must be balanced by activity. T'ai Chi movement is a moving meditation which provides the perfect balance to quiet sitting. Each activity enhances the other to move one forward toward complete spiritualization. When active, look for stillness in the activity. When engaged in quiet sitting meditation, find the creative animation in the stillness. In all things, combine and integrate all apparent opposites as undivided oneness.

Gentle Rhythmic Versus Hasty Violent Movements

Another universal principle revealed in T'ai Chi movement is the principle that sudden movement causes energy to stagnate, while gentle, rhythmic movement brings about its flow. Sudden movement must always stop quickly. Inevitably there is a pause or the inhibition of the energy flow. Similar to this is the principle that hasty action ultimately results in slowness because it quickly exhausts one's energy, while gentle rhythmic movement can be continued with great endurance. With this logic, we can understand that those who are violent can afford only one show of force at a time, and are weak in reality. Yet those who move in a gentle rhythm can keep going continually and prove to be the strongest. As another example, if a person decides to go to a distant place and tries to run all the way, he become exhausted before reaching his destination. But if he walks at a comfortable pace, he will eventually get there. This is a fundamental principle of T'ai Chi movement and indicates the "constant virtue" or constant quality inherent in gentle rhythmic movement.

The Circularity of All Natural Movement

The natural movement of everything in the universe follows a circular pattern. The earth spins on its axis as it orbits the sun. The sun, in turn, orbits the galactic center of the Milky Way. The Milky Way follows a circular pattern as it courses through the universe. Life itself consists of cycles, and the energies of the human organism also circulate through their microcosmic energy network. All of the movements of T'ai Chi are a series of circles which reflect this eternal, cosmic law.

The Law of Reversion
Everything in nature follows a cyclical process of growth and evolution. All things grow and develop and, after their peak has been reached, revert back to their source to regenerate again and again. The movement of evolution is not a linear process. Anything which continues in a straight line must eventually run out of power and come to an end. The multi-universe is able to continue its process of evolution eternally because it reverts to its source for regeneration before reaching the absolute end of its impetus. You may say that the energy is recycled.

This is an essential principle of T'ai Chi movement. In movement, one never extends one's body or energy completely because this will leave one with no energy in reserve. Instead, one goes only to a certain point, and then draws inward again to the center to gather one's energy. The movement is repeated, the force is recharged and the energy is recycled at the same time. This is called the law of reversion. In this way, the internal alchemy system of T'ai Chi movement expresses the principle of perpetual self-regeneration.

Most philosophies are merely intellectual concepts. However, Tao is not a concept and cannot be grasped conceptually. Taoist philosophy actually transcends the realm of philosophy because it can be clearly demonstrated through movement in daily life. T'ai Chi movement reveals to us all of the profound cosmic principles expounded in Lao Tzu's *Tao Teh Ching*. Lao Tzu frequently mentions the importance of avoiding fullness, because when the peak of fullness is reached, decline is inevitable. In T'ai Chi movement we learn how to control our energy to avoid fullness, thereby avoiding the peaks of growth and decay. One of the main goals in the practice of the Integral Way is to discover to discover and embrace the undivided root of the universe. With daily practice of T'ai Chi movement we may evolve to subtler and subtler levels of being and ultimately accomplish oneness with the Subtle Origin of all creation.

Chapter 6

The Application and Practice
of T'ai Chi Movement

Health

T'ai Chi movement is a self-healing method which can be practiced by anyone of any age in any condition of health. The therapeutic value of energy guidance exercise, which has had various names, has been recognized in China for thousands of years, but it is only recently that T'ai Chi movement has been acknowledged in the West as a means of restoring both physical and mental health. Consistent practice of T'ai Chi movement rectifies one's internal energies so effectively that the indirect result in many cases has been the curing of a wide variety of diseases, ranging from high blood pressure and ulcers to tuberculosis and heart disease. Its greatest health significance is its effectiveness in preventing disease by keeping the internal energies in a state of balance.

According to ancient integral medical theory, disease is the manifestation of energy disorder and aberration within the body. It is a state in which the various organs and the nervous system are functioning incorrectly or inadequately in a manner which is either too slow or fast, too weak or strong. When the energy flows through the channels unimpeded and the various organs are in a state of equilibrium, one is healthy. If the energy becomes imbalanced or blocked, disease manifests. Disease indicates that the energy flow needs to be corrected. Through the calmness and relaxation generated by T'ai Chi movement, the vitality which has been locked within a tense and imbalanced body is released and allowed to restore and sustain natural health.

From a different perspective, disease also occurs when the mind and body are out of harmony. The activity of the mind directly affects the dynamic processes taking place within the channel system, which in turn influences the physical form. The flow of energy within the body is influenced by the thoughts one thinks and the emotions one experiences. In order for the organism to function in optimum health, it is necessary for the emotions to shift from one to another throughout the day, and for the stream of thoughts to flow unimpeded.

If one particular emotion or mode of thinking is habitually emphasized, a particular organ may become overstimulated, causing depletion, imbalance and blockage within the channel system. Energy flows thus become altered or impeded, and certain organs may become congested with blood and chi while others receive an inadequate supply. This results in disease. The movements of T'ai Chi movement guide one's internal energies throughout the channels in such a way that a balance and order may be restored within the body.

The energy flow within the body is also influenced by the fact that when people are engaged in a physical activity, their minds are engaged in an unrelated activity. The mental and physical energies do not join forces, so to speak, to perform a particular task, but instead go off in different directions. This dichotomy is not the way nature intended the human organism to function, and this, too, causes energy disorder within the body.

The practice of T'ai Chi movement trains the mind to follow every detail of the body's actions. In this way, rather than literally scattering energy through unmindful physical activity, one is able to gather energy into one's organism. The peaceful mental atmosphere created by T'ai Chi movement allows negative thought patterns to dissolve and be replaced by positive, life-enforcing attitudes.

T'ai Chi movement helps the body absorb and utilize the energy from the food we eat. T'ai Chi movement accelerates the speed of energy generation within the body by producing gentle internal heat. This heat vaporizes the liquid energy derived from food in much the same way that the hot sun evaporates moisture from the earth. Because the energy from the food we eat is thus transformed from the liquid state to a vapor, it is much more easily transported and distributed to all of the organs of the body.

The human body can be likened to a tree. If the energy circulates to all parts of the tree, the entire tree is full of life. However, if one part of the tree does not receive its supply of energy, then that part withers.

In the human body, the energy must always be regenerated and it must be able to circulate freely to all parts of the body. In ordinary exercise, circulation is stimulated but energy is also burned up and lost in perspiration. Thus, one may generate energy but one also loses energy. In T'ai Chi movement the body may blossom in perfect condition without causing any perspiration. One's muscle tissue will be neither flaccid nor rigid, but full of energy like a ripe peach.

Through the burning and exhaustion of energy in daily activities, people grow old very fast. Energy conducting exercise is a means of refreshing one's energy and rejuvenating one's body. There are points within the body where energy is cultivated by practitioners of spiritual arts for the purpose of regeneration and rejuvenation. In man, the general point is located in the prostate gland and in women it is located in the thymus gland. The valley formed between the two buttocks in the case of men, and between the two breasts in the case of women, provides a natural focal point for the gathering of energy. The testicles or ovaries, the thymus and the pineal gland are the three areas most concerned with self-cultivation and correspond with the lower, middle and upper tan tien, respectively.

Ordinary exercise and sports may produce quick and shallow breathing which will cause more oxygen to enter the system. However, this type of exercise strains the heart and the lungs. In T'ai Chi movement, the heart is relaxed and the breathing is deep and full. This enables even more oxygen to enter the blood stream and utilizes the full capacity of the lungs. The rhythmic movements of T'ai Chi exercise produce friction between the organs, causing gentle warmth which strengthens and tonifies them.

Some forms of exercise will mobilize only a particular group of muscles, while Tai Chi movement brings all of the muscles of the body into play. T'ai Chi movement influences and benefits all systems of the body, in particular, the central nervous system, digestive system, respiratory system and endocrine system. The central nervous system extends from the base of the spine to the brain and is the most important system of the body. The function of the central nervous system is to receive information from both outside and inside of the body and transmit the body's actions and reactions to the brain. Through the practice of T'ai Chi movement, the central nervous system is gradually strengthened, developed and refined.

By training the mind and the body to be calm and relaxed, the brain and central nervous system may receive and transmit information more accurately and thoroughly. In T'ai Chi movement, the spine is always kept flexible and erect to allow the central nervous system to function effectively. When the spinal column is erect, blood and vital energy can be transmitted from the lower part of the body to the brain.

The expanding and contracting movements of T'ai Chi gentle exercise invigorate and tone the stomach and intestines, promoting good digestion. This expansion and contraction uses the full capacity of the lungs, strengthening the entire respiratory system. The deep and rhythmic breathing which is an intrinsic aspect of T'ai Chi movement causes the diaphragm to massage the internal organs and aids the circulation of fresh blood to the viscera. The circulation of fresh blood promotes the proper functioning of the endocrine system, which restores the chemical balance of the body. When the chemical balance of the body becomes rectified, metabolism improves.

T'ai Chi movement is not only for quiet people who are looking for a form of gentle exercise. It is also the best means of adjustment available for people who are very active physically and who want to key themselves down to a state of normal functioning. When a person is extremely overtired or tries to stop suddenly after engaging in very strenuous physical exertion, he may find that he is unable to rest. If a person forces oneself to rest in such a condition, physical damage will be caused. The same holds true when one is going from a state of deep meditation or relaxation to a state of normal activity. It is also very difficult to adjust.

T'ai Chi movement integrates all aspects of one's being and brings one into harmony with the natural law of the universe. Through the practice of T'ai Chi movement, one can learn to recognize and correct habits which violate the principles of the universe and cause ill health and dishar-mony. If one is unaware of the natural laws of the universe, it is easy to violate them and as a result, there is always a loss of balance and harmony, both internally and externally. If these imbalances persist, they destroy physical and mental health.

When an individual's energy system is in a state of disorder and imbalance, the corresponding energies mir-rored in the macrocosm reflect this disorder and lack of harmony. By balancing one's own internal energies and applying the natural laws discovered through T'ai Chi movement practice in daily life, a harmonious response from the universe naturally results. When every facet of one's life is an expression of natural law, one is spontaneously in tune with the universe.

Body-Mind Integration
Through the consistent practice of T'ai Chi gentle exercise, one may strengthen and integrate one's physical and mental functions. Generally, people either engage in mental activity and are oblivious to their bodies, or they engage in physical activity but their minds are wandering and not aware of what the body is doing. In this way, they create a split between body and mind, which are essentially one insepara-ble system.

Consciousness directly influences the energy flow and the general state of energy. The fact that this split is created and that body and mind do not function as one unit greatly impairs the ability to realize one's full potential. Nerve synapses atrophy from lack of use and vast areas of the brain lie dormant. Input from the external environment is inaccurately or incompletely transmitted to the brain, which in turn relays faulty messages as a response. As a result of this, the nervous system never fully develops and the awareness of reality, both internal and external, is vastly distorted.

At first, some people find T'ai Chi movements difficult to imitate, because they are unable to combine the internal with the external - which means they cannot combine the subtle energy of their minds and spirits with the grosser physical energy of their bodies. The purpose of T'ai Chi gentle exercise is not merely to achieve a certain standard of external movement and physical control, as in sports and dance. In order to perform T'ai Chi movement, the main requirement is that when the body moves, the chi and spirit also move.

This is achieved in the following manner: before starting to move, one empties the mind of all extraneous thought. Only when the mind is calm and unoccupied is one able to focus and direct it at will. When the movements are performed, they are done so very slowly. This allows the mind to pay attention to every detail of the body's movement. Physical strength is never employed to move the body. One combines the power of one's breath and subtle energy to propel the body. When the mind follows every detail of the body's activity, it affects the state of one's physical energy. The energy transforms from a distinct, individualized state to an undifferentiated, vaporized and electrical state.

The changing of physical energy to the vaporized and electrical states is a natural phenomenon in the body. The use of this specific type of movement creates the integration of energy. Not only do one's internal energies become integrated, but the internal energies also integrate with the energy of the environment in which one is practicing the movement. When one's energy is harmonized through movement, it is no longer merely physical energy, but is combined with the energy of mind and spirit as one integral whole. This is why it is said that T'ai Chi movement reunites all aspects of one's being in undivided oneness.

Gentle, Natural Rhythmic Movement

T'ai Chi movement is an intense training of both body and mind which enables them to function as one unit rather than separately. When defending oneself in martial arts, for example, one small mistake either in skill, temperament or disposition will cause one to be the loser. T'ai Chi movement trains a person to be calm, to have self-control, and to integrate these qualities with the internal techniques of fighting. The ability to achieve this integration can greatly benefit anyone who practices Kung Fu, boxing, Karate, or any other martial art. Through T'ai Chi movement, a professional fighter may learn more about control and balance in fighting. And even if a person who practices T'ai Chi movement has had no special training in self-defense, if the occasion should arise in which he needs to protect himself, he will spontaneously be prepared to do so. T'ai Chi movement practiced as a martial art relies on the projection of the chi toward one's opponent rather than on fighting technique. Strengthening oneself for fighting is not the direction of the Integral Way. The strength of health is of correct value to all generations.

Personality Development

No possession in the world is more valuable than a stable, pleasant personality. Despite the fact that there are many different techniques which attempt to improve the personality, it is rarely realized that personality is in essence an expression of the energy embodied by an individual. Modern psychological techniques may attempt to work on the mind through such means as positive thinking or various methods of mind control. Yet any technique which addresses itself only to the mind is dealing with form while ignoring substance.

For example, when "positive thinking" is stressed, two problems may be encountered. Positive thinking may keep a person in the realm of make-believe, preventing him or her from facing the reality of life; and excessive positivity which denies the potentiality of the opposite polarity may lead a person into difficulty by encouraging mental rigidity. The key to cultivating a balanced personality is to harmonize one's yin and yang elements. Since a person's personality is the expression of his energy, it follows that if a person's energy is rough, unrefined and unbalanced, his personality will express the same qualities. The way to improve the personality, then, is to transform the quality of one's energy, to refine the coarseness and equalize the imbalances.

By learning T'ai Chi movement, a person can effectively overcome all shortcomings of personality which are due to incompleteness and imbalance of energy. T'ai Chi movement accomplishes this without the need for any dogma or belief to control or restrain people. It improves the personality by refining and harmonizing the person's yin and yang energies, resulting in an even temperament and calm disposition. These qualities enable one to remain poised even through the most difficult situations. To be excessively negative is a form of madness, yet to be excessively positive is equally a form of madness. The way to avoid the duality of mind is through integrating all mental elements and functions. When the state of mental harmony is achieved, one's whole being is in consonance of its own accord.

Self-Cultivation

The first step of spiritual cultivation is to become aware of the existence of chi. Ordinarily, people's nervous systems are not sensitive enough to feel the chi that is either within their own bodies or outside of them. The energy within the human body exists in four states and is constantly changing from one phase of evolution to another. The four states are: solid, as bone and tissue; liquid, as blood, lymph, etc.; the vaporized or gas state; and the electrical state, which usually occurs in sexuality. All four states have both healthy and unhealthy manifestations.

When all of these states evolve and harmonize as one integrated and undifferentiated manifestation of energy, the ancient achieved ones refer to this as chi. Chi is invisible, but through the phenomena of life and death, its coming and going can be observed. Through the practice of T'ai Chi movement, an individual can develop his sensitivity so that he may experience and control the energy within the channel system of the body.

The spiritual process is essentially a process of refining one's energy to subtler and subtler states. T'ai Chi movement functions as a method by which this refinement may be accomplished so as to actualize the spiritualization of one's being. The Taoist Masters or ancient achieved ones of antiquity exposed the fact that there are three steps comprising the process of spiritualization. The first is the refinement of physical essence or sexual energy into mental energy. The second is the refinement of mental energy into spiritual energy. The third is the refinement of spiritual energy in order to unite oneself with the Subtle Origin of the universe, which constitutes the birth of an individual into the Immortal Realm. T'ai Chi gentle exercise is a practical approach to achieving this goal.

There are three basic styles or grades of T'ai Chi movement which enable one to refine all three categories of energy. The first style or grade is called the "Style of Wisdom," the "Earth Style" or "Gentle Path T'ai Chi movement" in which the energy is concentrated in the lower tan tien below the navel. This style corresponds with the physical plane. The popular Yang style exemplifies the same principle as the Earth Style; however, the original Earth Style is the genuine expression of the principle. This style refines the energy from the food we eat and the air we breathe and transforms it into physical essence. The Earth Style is suitable to be performed by either the beginner or the long-trained practitioner as a means of energy adjustment. This style is appropriate for spring or summer. The spring especially is a wonderful time to gather the warmth radiated from the earth.

The second style of T'ai Chi is called the "Style of Harmony," the "Mankind Style" or "Sky Journey T'ai Chi movement." It is the genuine expression of this principle and also illustrated by the more ancient Chen style. In this style the energy corresponds with the mental plane and is concentrated in the middle tan tien. This style is suitable to be practiced in the autumn.

The third style is called the "Style of Integration," the "Heaven Style" or "Infinite Expansion T'ai Chi movement" in which the energy is concentrated in the general yang channel in the back and neck. This is the ancient esoteric style and artful training to attune one's metabolism and rejuvenate one's internal secretions. In this style, the spirit centers the whole constitution of the being. This style accelerates the circulation, bodily secretions and excretion of toxins. It helps the metabolism of people of all ages, especially after middle age. However, quite a bit of training is required because it is the most difficult style to learn well. It is preferable that one begins to learn this style when one is young and the body is supple.

Through these styles of T'ai Chi one can understand the body, mind and spirit, and bring about their reintegration. However, if one does not learn or develop the internal alchemy systems of these forms, they remain merely a superficial shell. Until just one generation ago, the internal methods of T'ai Chi movement were carefully guarded secrets, the essence of natural spiritual culture. These secrets were passed only through family heritage or esoteric traditions. With much devotion, and under strict and precise instruction, one may learn and master T'ai Chi movement and benefit from this treasure of spiritual culture.

Practice
The basic requirements for the practice of T'ai Chi movement are calmness, concentration, relaxation, gradualness,

balance, symmetry, empty mindedness, naturalness, rhythm and suppleness. The following adaptations of traditional T'ai Chi movement classics elucidate the practice of this art:

> *T'ai Chi, the ultimate form, arises out of wu chi, the Undivided Oneness. It is the origin of movement and stillness, and the Mother of yin and yang. In movement it generates, in stillness it returns. Neither exceeding nor falling short, T'ai Chi moves in bending and stretching. When one yields to a hard force, this is called 'moving around it.' When one tackles with a hard force, this is called 'sticking with it.'*
>
> *When the other's movement comes quickly, respond quickly. When the other's movement comes slowly, follow slowly. In myriad changing situations, the principle is the same.*
>
> *From familiarity with the exercise comes a gradual realization and understanding of energy. From the understanding of energy there comes spiritual illumination. Yet only after long, diligent practice will this sudden seeing through be achieved.*
>
> *Empty and alert, still and quiet. The breath sinks into the lower tan tien. Not inclined, not leaning. Suddenly concealing, suddenly manifesting. When an intruding weight comes to my left, my left is empty. When an intruding weight comes to my right, then my right disappears.*
>
> *Looking up, the other feels my height. Looking down, other feels my depth. Advancing, he feels the distance lengthening. Retreating, he is more crowded. A small bird cannot take off, because there is no solid part to ascend from. Nor can a single fly land. The opponent does not know where the energy is changing in me, but I alone know where the opponent's force is located.*
>
> *When great heroes are without match, it is because of all of these factors. There are many other techniques of combat. Whatever their differences, they all nevertheless rely on the strong to overcome the weak, and the slow to give in to the fast. Yet as far as the*

strong beating the weak, the slow giving in to the fast,
such things derive from natural abilities and do not
have to be studied. When 'four ounces move a thousand pounds' it is obviously not a matter of strength.
When an old man can withstand many young men,
how can it be through accomplishment of speed?

Stand as a poised scale. In action be as a wheel.
With the center of your gravity displaced to one side,
you can be fluid. If you are 'double heavy,' with your
weight evenly distributed on both feet, you become
stagnant. Often one encounters someone who even
after many years of study has not achieved proper
development and is still subdued by others. This is
because he has not realized the fault of 'double heaviness.' To avoid this fault, one must know yin and
yang. To stick is also to move away and to move
away is also to stick. Yin does not leave yang and
yang does not leave yin. Yin and yang always complement each other. To understand this is necessary
in order to understand energy. When one understands
energy, the more one practices, the more wonderful
will be his development. One comprehends in silence
and experiences in feeling, until gradually one may act
at will.

There is the traditional advice to deny self and to
yield to the other, but many have misunderstood this
to mean to abandon the near and to seek the far.
Only a true Master has the skill to demonstrate this
principle. A mistake of inches but an error of a thousand leagues. Therefore, the student needs to pay
careful heed to what is said.

(adapted from The Treatise on T'ai Chi Chuan,
attributed to Wang, Chung-Yueh the foremost pupil
of Zhan, San Fong)

The following is adapted from A Discussion of the
Practice of T'ai Chi Ch'uan, a traditional text, which is sometimes attributed to Master Zhan, San Fong who lived in the
13th century:

When one begins to move, the entire body should be light and flexible, and the movement must be continuous. The chi should be expanded with vitality and the mind tranquil. Do not allow gaps, unevenness or discontinuities. Your feet are the root of energy, which passes through the legs, is controlled by the waist, and finally emerges through the fingers. Your feet, legs and waist need to be coordinated so that in moving forward and backward you have good control of time and space. Without this control of time and space in all movements - up, down, left, right, forward and backward - your body will be in disorder and the fault must be sought in the waist and legs. All of these principles concern the will rather than merely the external.

When there is up, there must be down; when there is left, there must be right. The will to go up implies the will to go down. For if upon lifting an opposing force you add the idea of pushing it down, then the root of your opposition is broken and without doubt you will overcome it quickly.

The empty and solid can be clearly distinguished. Each physical situation by nature has an empty side and a solid side. This is true of every physical situation. Let there be continuity in the movements of the entire body. Let there be not the slightest break.

The mind moves the chi calmly and naturally, directing it deeply inward; then it can be gathered into the bones and marrow. The chi moves the entire being smoothly and continuously; then the form can easily follow the mind. If your energies are vitalized, then there is no problem about being sluggish and heavy. To accomplish this the spine needs to be erect as if the head were suspended. The mind and chi must move flexibly in order to achieve smoothness and roundness of movement. This is accomplished by the interchange of yin and yang.

To concentrate the energy one must sink one's center of gravity, maintain looseness and quietude, and focus one's energy in a single direction. To stand

one must remain centrally poised, calm and expanded,
and one can thus protect himself from all sides. Move
the energy like a delicate string of pearls so there is no
place that the energy does not reach. Refine your
essence to become like flawless steel so there is no
obstruction it cannot destroy.

The appearance is as a hawk catching a rabbit; the
spirit, as a cat watching a mouse. In resting be as still
as a mountain; in movement be like a river. Store the
energy as if drawing a bow. Issue the energy as if
releasing the arrow. Through the curve seek the
straight. First store then release. The energy issues
from the spine. Steps follow changes in the form. To
withdraw is to release. To release is to withdraw. To
break is to continue. Back and forth must have folds,
no straight path in either case, in order to prepare and
gather the energy. Advancing and retreating must
have turns and changes.

Through what is greatly soft one achieves what is
greatly strong. If one is able to inhale and exhale,
then one can be light and flexible. Breathing must be
nourished without impediment, no holding of the
breath and no forcing it, then no harm will come. The
energy must be bent like a bow and stored, then you
will always have more than you need. The mind
orders, the chi goes forth as a banner, the waist takes
the command. First seek to stretch and expand;
afterwards seek to tighten and collect; then one attains
integrated development.

It is said:

First the mind, afterwards the body. The abdomen
is relaxed, the chi is gathered into the bones, the spirit
is at ease and the body quiet. At every moment be
totally conscious.

It must be remembered:

As one part moves, all parts move; if one part is
still, all parts are still. Pull and move, go and come,
the chi goes to the back and is gathered in the spine,

making the spirit firm and leisurely manifesting calm without. Step as a cat walks. Use force as if pulling silk. Throughout the body concentrate on the spirit and not on the chi. To concentrate on the chi causes stagnancy. To be with chi, or holding the breath, is to be without strength. To be without chi, moving the breath and allowing it to flow freely, one can be really strong. The breath is like a cart's wheel. The waist is like its axle.

(adapted from the *Essential Principles for Practicing T'ai Chi Ch'uan*, by W.S. Wu, 1812-1880)

Chapter 7

A Simple and Practical Emotional Life

Human life is supported by various energies. We obtain our energy from the food we eat as well as from the physical and subtle universal environment. When energy is able to follow its natural function, it circulates in a continuous movement through the human body, through all the other living beings and manifestations, and throughout the entire universe. The energy external to our bodies is referred to as universal energy. The energy growing inside of us may be called our individual energy. Even though the external energy of the universe is generally not under our direct control, we can depend on the normal course of nature and live within the order of the universal energy.

The energy within us, on the other hand, may be guided by the individual to a certain extent. The energy within us manifests as physical energy, emotional energy, mental energy and spiritual energy. These energies are essentially one, but because of the necessities and attractions of living in this world, the one energy manifests differently in order to function in the various aspects of life. Depending on each person's disposition, these energies may manifest positively and in a focused, creative way, or negatively and in distractions. For example, sometimes even if one has something constructive at hand with which to be busy, one's energy may still drift away from one's work.

Emotion is one manifestation of energy in our lives. It has a close connection with the physical and mental energies. A stimulation of the body may cause an emotional reaction like joy, happiness, sadness, pain, agony and so forth. Likewise, through mental stimulation the emotions will immediately manifest physically in laughter, weeping, frowning, sighing or in subtle changes in the body's chemistry. Emotional energy has a lower frequency than mental functions like observation, understanding, reflection, contemplation and so on. In many emotions, especially strong negative emotions, the energy is almost as gross as physical energy. Emotion lies on the very margin between body and mind, and is a transferable and transmissible medium. We can be influenced emotionally by other people and by our environment, and in less perceptible ways by the chemical changes in our bodies and by the subtle universal energy cycles.

Emotional Balance

When one is unaware of the subtle influences which affect one's moods, it is easy to become dominated by one's emotions. Then one tends to identify completely with one's emotions and they are no longer just one component of life. This reveals itself in statements such as "I am happy," "I am sad" and so forth. If one identifies with one's emotions, one is unable to spontaneously respond with the appropriate normal expression in the arising situations. As a result, the whole being of a person is molded by the emotional aspect of his or her energy structure.

If people are unaware of their emotional imbalance, they may content themselves with mental consolations such as "I am entitled to feel however I feel. This is the way I am." Or they may fall into the opposite extreme and forcefully suppress their emotions, denying the positive and healthy function of their feelings and normal reactions. This violates one's true nature and occurs frequently in traditions which practice asceticism.

As long as one is unaware of the possibility of evolving beyond a trying emotional life, one will either deny one's healthy emotional expression or constantly struggle with emotional ups and downs. In either case, one usually experiences repeated defeats.

A positive approach to one's emotional life is the conscious guiding and directing of one's internal energy. In order to transcend the emotional approach to life, we have to conduct our energy consciously and appropriately. Through the practice of meditation one may accomplish the continuous circulation of one's internal energy and, as a consequence, experience a calm mind and a profound change in one's emotions and reactions to life. With a peaceful and clear mind, we can recognize that most of our emotional disturbances occur without any real reason. An emotional disorder may be stimulated by something of little or no importance. But in order to justify one's emotional upset, one may unconsciously exaggerate and dramatize any small incident and transform it into a severe problem.

It is helpful to observe one's emotional reactions with a clear and centered mind because they reflect the state of one's physical and mental energy. A person with balanced energy will manifest appropriate and harmonious emotional reactions.

The healthy emotional expression of a human being has two primary elements which are signs of natural self-discipline; his innate qualities of self-control and self-respect. Both these attributes are rooted in serenity. Serenity unfolds itself as a calm inner happiness, and it is enduring and completely independent of external conditions. Self-control and self-respect combined manifest as the ability to be conscious of, or sensitive to, transgressions toward oneself and other human beings as well as toward all creations. These fundamental and innate qualities of our nature need to be cultivated continuously to remain unaffected by artificial or environmental influences.

Ordinary happiness expresses itself as a release of emotional tension, and is really a dissipation of energy. One actually expends energy with the outburst of happiness. If experiences follow which can be interpreted as negative, this increases one's susceptibility to being overwhelmed. Ordinary happiness is only a momentary and occasional experience.

Self-respect in the ordinary sense is based on the self-esteem derived from one's accomplishments, social status and other external criteria. It is combined with rigidity and dogma, and depends on the evaluation of someone external to oneself. Ordinary self-respect denies the need to release our internal emotional pressures and stiffens our natural capability to be sensitive to infringements in our relationships and in our environment.

Integral self-cultivation employs certain methods for the restitution of one's natural emotional quality of serenity. Deep meditation and reflection lead one to self-discovery, and the practice of "self-release" gives one the experience of absolute oneness. Both release the tensions we have accumulated in the past and free us from worries abut the future. The practice of these methods will gradually dissolve all obstructions in one's energy flow. At the same time, one extends one's being into the subtle universal realms and reaches profound awareness. One connects one's being with the whole continuum of time and space in an absolute way.

Absolute happiness and healthy sensitivity can be realized only through true self-discovery and through self-release. It is important, however, to refrain from any ambition in one's self-cultivation, as it will have detrimental effects. Only self-control and self-respect further one's spiritual evolution. If we combine sincerity with self-control we will stay free from entanglement in worldly and spiritual illusions. Likewise, sincerity combined with self-respect will guide our emotions appropriately.

As a result we will reach true self-awareness and mastery over dissipation. Respect creates receptivity to higher frequencies of energy and can raise one from the ordinary relative realm to the absolute realm of existence. If one strives for happiness alone, one inevitably falls into moral depravity and loses one's well-being. By restoring and invigorating the natural awareness in the heart of our being, we transform life into a sacred expression of our unity with all aspects of the universe. Unity and harmony characterize the way we experience reality when we adhere to our innate qualities of self-discipline or self-control. Then we respect our own being and neither violate nor scatter our physical, emotional mental and spiritual energies whether we are alone or in the company of others.

Psychological Health

The emotional approach to life can cause great harm. The cherishing of emotional love usually has suffering as its consequence. Emotional agitation in politics or in religious activities results in disturbances of one's mental clarity and blind zealotry. Emotional allurement combined with cultural, social or commercial purposes destroys the balance in people's lives and personalities. Without a deep recognition of one's true nature, one is incapable of maintaining one's emotional independence and developing wisdom, and one is left in a continuous struggle with one's psychological problems.

Two common psychological imbalances are the emotional demands for love and respect. People who do not feel love within themselves demand love from others, and similarly, people who lack self-respect suffer the psychological pressure to prove that they are worthy of respect and may resort to unusual behavior in order to do so. When one has reached true self-awareness, one realizes one's own intrinsic value and is not dependent on someone else's love and respect, or on high professional and social positions; however, one does not deny these either. Psychological problems are merely a deviation from one's true nature and a weakness caused by an undisciplined and scattered mind, the dissipation of one's energy and the loss of self-respect. Psychological problems are therefore each person's own creation. People who lack self-awareness and self-discipline have no foundation for virtue and strength of character.

The integral definition of self-discipline is to have respect for oneself in all aspects of life. It is realized through appropriate action and behavior, and extends to all activities, including one's work and even so-called trivialities. Some examples of appropriate behavior are to sit upright, to walk steadily, to be mindful of machines, and to make them work well for oneself instead of relying on them blindly. Man needs to respect all of creation and to take responsibility for all his actions, his thoughts and his spoken words, because all these factors create the reality of his life.

The pure natural attributes of love and freedom cannot be enjoyed without the two aspects of serenity: self-control and self-respect. True love is an expression of one's human-heartedness, and true freedom lies in the realization of harmony with the universal law. Many people engage in emotional indulgence and call these shallow feelings love, or they demand freedom in love and mistake the mere dissipation of their energy for true freedom. Self-cultivation aims at the elimination of emotional indulgence and dissipation through the emphasis of self-discipline and self-mastery.

The highest integral principle in regard to our emotional life is the recognition of our own intrinsic value. When we are aware of our intrinsic value, we are able to restore and maintain a balanced personality and do not depend on any external evaluation and acceptance. By relying only on what we truly are, we develop the positive elements of our being and eliminate our negativity. One respects other people and all creations, but does not sacrifice one's inner peace for disrespectful demands placed on oneself by others. One recognizes the intrinsic value of all beings and things and has compassion for those who have not yet awakened to their own true nature.

Our inner awareness is our spiritual light. Spirituality has nothing to do with emotional flattery or religious veneration of an authoritarian god or idol. Emotional demands and dependence do not promote spiritual growth. All of our motives, actions, relationships and concepts of value should be inspired by our own being and guided by our awareness.

Living a life of truth does not require that one becomes a leader of society or display ambition for spiritual achievement. Leading an ordinary balanced life is a great accomplishment in itself. Radiating one's inner harmony and positively influencing one's environment is a real service to the world and to oneself.

Focusing one's attention merely on the external world to aggrandize oneself or to act like a savior leaves one weak at one's center and open to the influence of the culture or society, or to one's own emotions. The use of aggressive emotional force may result in external accomplishments, but does not provide the real power of self-control. People who depend upon their emotional force will despair when they are faced with a crisis. If one has reached true self-awareness, one's personality remains unchanged under any circumstance, and one's inner peace enables one to overcome any obstacle.

The Principle of Appropriateness

The classic integral teachings suggest that one adheres to "The Principle of Appropriateness" in one's behavior:

> The great nature of the universe has endowed human beings with its very own nature. Living in accord with nature is called the Way of Life. To follow the Way closely is called self-cultivation.
>
> The Way is absolute. It may not be deviated from for an instant. If it could be deviated from it would not be the absolute Way. One of nature does not wait until he sees himself go beyond the Way to be cautious, nor till he knows that he has violated the Way to be apprehensive.
>
> There is nothing more apparent than what is usually thought to be the secret of one's feelings and nothing more manifest than the minutest of one's moods. Therefore one of nature tends his life with great care because he has the power to do either harm or good even when alone.
>
> Rejoicing, anger, sorrow, happiness, worry, anxiety, frustration, love, hate and so forth are the elements of emotion. If any one of these is over-manifested, it will destroy the normalcy of the entire being. Likewise rain, snow, frost, fog, heat, cold, wind and so forth are the transformations of weather. If one of them over-manifests it will upset the normalcy of the seasons and there will be calamity. When each is manifested in accordance with the circumstance, it is normal and

appropriate. If one over-reacts, it is called sickness and destruction. When human beings lose the normalcy of their true nature, just like when the weather goes beyond the bounds of normalcy, there must be disaster.

When there is no stirring of pleasure, anger, sorrow or joy, the mind has a state of harmonious equilibrium. If these feelings have not been stirred and act in their proper measure, the state of creative appropriateness ensues. Harmonious equilibrium is the root from which all creation springs forth, and creative appropriateness is the universal way which all creation follows.

Let the state of harmonious equilibrium and creative appropriateness exist in perfection and an order of peace and creativeness will prevail through the universe in which all living beings and things will be nourished and flourish.

One of nature embodies the course of harmonious equilibrium and creative appropriateness. One who has lost the Way acts against the course of nature. One of nature embodies the course of nature because he is aware of his own true nature. One who has lost the Way acts against the course of nature because he has no self-discipline.

One of true wisdom chooses the Way and whenever he gains knowledge of what is good, he clasps it firmly to his breast and does not lose it.

One may rule a family, a state or a kingdom well. One may decline high positions and bountiful emoluments. One may walk on sharp knives with naked feet. But one may not so easily adhere to the course of harmonious equilibrium toward oneself and creative appropriateness toward the external world.

Complete virtue is in accordance with nature. Rare are the ones who can realize it. I know why the Way does not prevail among people. The knowing regulate themselves too much, the smart go beyond it and the stupid cannot reach it. I know why the Way is not understood. The ones of talent and virtue go beyond it and the untalented and unvirtuous do not reach it.

All people eat and drink but there are few who can practice the principle of appropriateness in eating and drinking. People think they are wise, but when they are driven forward and trapped in a net or pitfall, they know not how to escape. This indicates that they are insensitive to the universal law of subtle energy response. People think they are wise, but they cannot adhere to the course of harmonious equilibrium and creative appropriateness for even a round month.

The Way is not far from a person, but when he searches for the Way outside of himself, it evades him.

In hewing an ax handle, the pattern in one's mind is not far off from the real one. One grasps an ax handle to hew a new one, but if one looks from one to the other, they will not be exactly the same. Therefore, one of nature demands to be treated by others according to his own inherent nature of completeness. He does not look for an external artificial pattern to be forced on himself or others.

When one cultivates oneself to the utmost principle of harmony, one follows the universal Way of life.

Practicing archery is like the Way of nature. When the archer misses the bull's eye of the target, he turns back and looks within himself for the cause of the failure.

Chapter 8

The Integral Science of Ethics

The values held by former generations seem artificial and meaningless to many people in the present time. As a result, previously accepted codes of ethics have been discarded, and no new relevant and trustworthy guidelines have been introduced to fill the void created by their absence. Throughout most countries on earth, confusion and great disharmony are prevalent. Personal and social unrest demands a standard to live by which is relevant to contemporary life and in accordance with universal law. Human civilization seems to be at the peak of its development technologically, yet the fibre of most societies is crumbling, and the culturally created relative morality and artificial ethics are not a sufficient foundation upon which people may build their lives.

We are limited in our ability to control our environment. The area in which we really can effect positive change in our life and in society is within the realm of consciousness. Our consciousness is a continually developing container in which all the events of our life are held and formed. Before one is born, one's mind is pure and formless. As the pressures of life shape and structure our mind, they create rigid and distorted thought patterns. In this way we lose our ability to perceive and experience the reality of our lives. If one can reconstruct one's mind and restore its original, positive and innocent quality, the events of one's life, which are in essence one's own mental projection and expression, will also be positive.

The Universal Law of Subtle Energy Response
The fortune and misfortune in our lives is self-created and results from our ignorance and violation of the universal law of subtle energy response. It does not ensue from external events, as most people assume. Subtle energy responds to man's energy through the mechanics of resonance, and

depending on the energy he embodies, it finds its expression in positive or negative events.

The response of the subtle energy may affect the acting person directly or through a medium which suffers the consequences of his actions. The mystical net of energy responses, also called destiny, is wide-meshed, and the subtle energy does not necessarily respond immediately to the energy we project. But the principle of the universal law of subtle energy response applies to all creation and extends its influence over the whole continuum of time and space in all its transformations.

The Principle of Appropriateness in Ethics
The understanding of the universal law of subtle energy response and the principle of appropriateness provide the basis for the integral science of ethics. The principle of appropriateness relates to the projection of our energy, and suggests the use of the appropriate amount of energy in the appropriate place in the appropriate time. It stems from the observation that our intrinsic nature or energy manifests appropriately in the realm of daily life of its own virtue, if we remain in harmonious relation with the real matters of our life and the nature of the universe.

The rules of right or wrong conduct, which are commonly used to regulate people's behavior, do not regard the specific time and circumstances of an event. Thus one may strongly insist on something being right or wrong without considering the reality of the situation.

The principle of appropriateness is expressed in the *I Ching* as the way of balancing the yin — — and yang ——— energies. Originally, human behavior was not classified as right or wrong, but merely varied according to the situation. It was either a weak — — or a strong ——— expression of human energy, as symbolized by certain arrangements of broken and unbroken lines.

Right and wrong cannot be defined through language. Language merely serves as an interpretation of a situation and labels it right or wrong. Language holds no authority to place judgement; the reality of the matter or situation stands for itself. The *I Ching*, therefore, delineates the subject matter in the form of the diagrams of the yin/yang system, and uses language as a supplementary means of description.

The reality of ethics and physics are actually one. The intention of the integral sciences is to demonstrate the identicalness of metaphysical and physical phenomena, the oneness of the reality of spirit and the reality of matter, the oneness of spirituality and ordinariness in our lives. The human mind creates duality, but through integral knowledge and practices, one may reintegrate the apparent dualities in one's life and experience oneness.

Virtue

Virtue is the creative power originating from the nature of the universe. The constancy of universal nature gives us the opportunity to develop discernment toward ourselves and all manifestations, toward those appearing as creativity as well as those displaying themselves as inertia. The nature and virtue of the universe remains positive, creative, constructive, productive and affirmative under any circumstance. Human beings have the potential to develop their ability to know and experience the constant virtue behind the changeable, superficial phenomena created by the universal energy cycles.

Tao is infinite and formless, but in the physical universe it is recognizable as constant virtue, as teh. When any part of creation succumbs to the movement of its internal or of the external energy cycles, it ceases to exist. Man in particular has difficulties in finding contentment and sufficiency within his own being, and leaves his intrinsic nature in the pursuit of being something or someone else. The serenity of our profound nature has been disrupted, therefore we die not when we physically cease to breathe, but rather in each moment that we stray from our profound nature.

If one cultivates and reunites oneself with the Tao, one follows the eternal Way and embodies the constancy and virtue of the universe. Tao is the original source of all life and all mechanical forces in the universe. When we distinguish ourselves from Tao through the creation of thoughts, we cease to live in harmony.

If one does not cultivate the internal and external expression of one's virtue in order to harmonize oneself with the universal law and to evoke the response of the positive energies of the universe, one's thinking and behavior will be motivated and manipulated by external as well as internal influences from the lower realms of existence. These influences will create disorder in our lives if we allow them to establish themselves as our reality.

Achieving Harmony - Internally and Externally

External influences consist of our immediate environment and of celestial influences. Our immediate environment is our family, friends, and co-workers, our society, and our geographical location. As we grow up we are subjected to emotional influences and mental conditioning, and all the problems inherent in the environment in which our socialization takes place. Our behavior is determined by the pressure and stress in our environment, and we are compelled to actions which we would not take under normal circumstances. With emotional balance and mental clarity, one can react directly even in the most difficult situations and can follow the universal nature of productiveness and creativity rather than indulge in destructive tendencies. If we allow external influences to intrude into our being, we lose our personal gravity, and as a result, our energy floats upward and we cannot remain grounded and centered in our three tan tien. Then we will take actions which are beyond our normal measure, and problems and accidents will be unavoidable.

When one's energy is balanced and one's mind clear, then one's will is resolute. Conversely, if one's energy is unbalanced, one is easily manipulated by someone with negative energy or through one's own unclear mind. One is therefore moved to act without real desire and even against one's conscience and wisdom and one becomes dominated by unconscious psychological imitation. This tendency is exploited commercially and politically, especially through the media, and it is also found in religious emotionalism and educational approaches.

The sun is the most consequential of the celestial influences because it is the earth's major source of energy. It supports life on earth and determines the growth, the strength and the daily energy cycles of all life. The energy of the moon, which follows a very distinguishable cycle of waxing and waning, plays a significant role in our intellectual and emotional life, and influences sexual desire and women's menstruation as well as the ocean tides. The full moon may cause restlessness and impulsiveness, but can also make people very energetic. It is a good time for cultivation and creative expression.

These natural universal influences reflect on our complex and stressful contemporary life style. By developing sensitivity to celestial influences, we can adjust our lives to be in harmony with nature. Through the understanding of both our own and universal energy cycles, we can harmonize our internal energies with the universal energies. Integral cosmology is a topic dealing with specific knowledge and techniques related to universal energies.

The elements which influence us internally are our mind, our desires and our impulses. The human mind can be an instrument of insight, inspiration and ingenuity, and can assist us in our self-development and self-discovery, but it can also be our greatest enemy. Our beliefs and values bind our mind to the realm of dualistic vision. The original nature of the human mind, however, is absolute. The questions of good or bad and right or wrong are merely a creation of the dualistic mind.

Only one energy exists in the absolute realm, but in the relative realm it can manifest appropriately or inappropriately. This distinction lies still within the realm of pure morality. When this distinction is complicated through artificial concepts about behavior, it then becomes ordinary morality and may become an obstacle to the experience of life. For example, when a man marries a woman, it is appropriate behavior and a question of pure morality. But when their marriage is determined or prevented by religious denomination or social discrimination, then it is a question of ordinary morality. Mental conditioning and concepts will prevent one's spontaneous and harmonious expression and divert one's energy to manifest as internal emotional pressures.

Using the mind resembles using a camera. If one can achieve absolute oneness with what appears as the multiformity of the world, one can unify the fragments of one's mind and focus one's mental camera instantly to receive a clear and accurate picture of reality. This is the correct function of the mind.

Desire, an energy manifestation closely related to physical and mental energy, is frequently blamed as the cause of man's problems. But trouble ensues only when desire is out of balance with the higher functions of the mind and serves the lower ones instead. The natural order is for the lower attributes of the mind to serve the higher, and for the mind to be the servant of the spirit or subtle energy which is the master over all aspects of a human being and all creation. The opposite order, however, predominates in most people's minds and is the reason for their problems and degeneration. Their minds are subdued by blind desire, which is a manifestation of physical energy.

When one's physical energy is overly strong in relation to one's mental and spiritual energy, one experiences difficulties in maintaining the equilibrium and harmony of one's being. Out of physical desire one may lose one's calmness and clarity of mind and be compelled to act against one's better judgement. Imbalance will also result when one's idealism is not in accord with the practical reality of one's life. The pursuit of mental as well as physical desire will disturb the equilibrium of the mind and prevent its effective and appropriate functioning.

The mechanics of desire are covert. A certain desire may not be filled and may unconsciously trigger the activation of a different desire, and one may be motivated to satisfy an apparently inexplicable desire. Or one may not be equipped with the material means to satisfy one's desires and may therefore resort to inappropriate actions. When pure intelligence and wisdom rule one's mind, one's energy circulates smoothly throughout the body and subtle energy systems.

Impulse, which is also closely connected with the body and mind, is a strong motivating factor. It may be the direct response to a stimulus or may carry out the order indicated by desire. The quality of impulse is very sudden and immediate, and is therefore difficult to control. One tends to be impulsive especially when one's physical energy is unstable. Impulse can spring from any aspect of the mind and may be motivated by desires of physical or intellectual nature. In itself, impulse is neither positive nor negative. Difficulties arise only out of blind impulsiveness.

Blind impulsiveness is behavior which is involuntary compelled by the needs and desires of the body and mind. If we follow our biological impulses to eat and procreate blindly, we will encounter many mishaps. Our hormonal secretions may stimulate the physical desire to procreate and the psychological suggestion to find a sexual partner, and we may neglect the importance of a spiritual connection with our partner; or this desire may be diverted to an unnormal desire for food or material possessions, or manifest as over-exertion and other inappropriate behavior. When the expression of one's desire is guided by one's spirit, it is transformed in spontaneously correct and appropriate behavior and one is able to take full responsibility for the consequences of one's actions.

Spirit is the essence of our being. If spirit is the directing energy in our life, then our desires and impulses are balanced and harmonious and fulfill their natural function as expressions of the positive, creative and constructive nature of the universe. In the absolute ream of spirit, the mind has the positive function of a highly sensitive transmitter and receiver, and is capable of spontaneous knowledge without previous experience of or the distinction between good or bad. Before one is able to receive spiritual enlightenment, on must be absolutely virtuous, practice the principle of appropriateness, and display one's innate moral qualities of selflessness and responsibleness. If one does not have the foundation of true and pure ethics, any spiritual teaching will be without influence on the reality of one's life. Spiritual knowledge and techniques alone may create mental stimulation, but are merely another form of LSD or mental opiate, and have nothing to do with the truth of spirit and the reality of life.

People generally believe that the mind is the place where they can enjoy freedom even in difficult situations. But this is a delusion. One attains freedom only through total liberation. Only the absolute mind is able to be a clear channel for the expansion of spiritual awareness and the experience of freedom. When we evolve beyond the realm of the dualistic and conditioned mind, then we will experience spiritual stability and live in harmony, simplicity and true freedom. This is the goal of integral self-cultivation.

Chapter 9

Spiritual Arts

Self-Cultivation

There are many different spiritual practices. Some use substitutes to move your focus away from a troubled mind. There are also effective methods by which one may develop oneself directly to pacify one's mind. All of these effective methods are intended to cause a response of the universal law, but their results and spiritual levels vary. Some people fail to recognize the ultimate reality of life and merely honor superficial rituals and beautifully decorated altars, churches or temples. This creates the basis for religious prejudice and vanity, and circumvents real spirituality.

Many people practice yoga or meditation. Their intention is to further their health, to have a different experience of life or to achieve personal growth. Yet they may neglect the basic universal law of life and actually damage their well-being. Also, not all of these systems were designed according to the Way of nature.

There are two correct ways to cultivate one's energy. One way develops one's personal nature and ability to connect with universal law through movement in meditation, and is based on the principle of harmony. The other way is the practice of the principle of spontaneity during one's cultivation of quietude. Then one's energy naturally becomes coherent with the universal law, and inspirations and insights occur. These experiences are spontaneous and natural, and cannot be learned by conforming to a particular routine or mental framework. Nevertheless, it is most important not to mistake uncontrolled, aberrated behavior as spontaneity.

Spontaneity is the highest principle in spiritual cultivation and life. After man evolves to the absolute level of being, his breathing may cause wind, his sneeze a rain storm, his anger a fire, and his shaking an earthquake. Man's daily activities evoke a response of universal law, but the real power comes from spontaneity as it is achieved and developed by real Masters or achieved ones. When practicing the Integral Way, one makes the important discovery that a human being is not a single, separate and isolated phenomenon. Rather, one experiences all aspects of life as interconnected and interrelated with the vast universe. In the dimension of time, what happens now is inevitably linked with the past and the future. In the dimension of space, everything one does either directly or indirectly influences the sphere of the universe to which one is connected, and a response appears in one's actions or mental projections.

The ancient spiritual teachings are rich in knowledge and techniques for the arrangement and development of a human's energy. Through the use of cultivation, a man or woman can serve oneself and others. Practitioners of the Integral Way refine their energy until it becomes as subtle as the pivotal energy of the universe. Any self-cultivation method applied at the appropriate time and in the appropriate place will cause the appropriate enduring result. In this way an achieved one practices the propriety of the natural Way of life as a balanced and fully developed universal being.

The simple life style consists of many fundamental practices. The easiest and most important practices are early rising and retiring, the practice of serenity in sitting and moving, heeding one's words, the avoidance of excessive sexual activity and indulgence in foods, and the abstinence from engagement in unnecessary activities. Each aspect is significant in the refinement of one's energy and needs to be attended to conscientiously and consistently.

The very early morning is the best time for self-cultivation. This time affords one deep peace and quiet before the daily activities begin, and also enables one to gather the beneficial, tranquil energies which are available only during the very early morning hours. This practice enhances one's health as well as one's spiritual growth. Spending time outdoors among the energies of the trees and other plants early in the morning is revitalizing and calming to one's entire being. Retiring before ten o'clock at night enable ones to rise early. Five to six hours sleep each night are sufficient for an adult; too much sleep will cause stagnation in the body's energy flow. Sleeping in a sitting position or in one of the sleeping postures for spiritual cultivation enables one to accumulate subtle energy while sleeping.

Quiet sitting meditation may be practiced for fifteen minutes in the beginning and gradually prolonged. In meditation one gathers energy and obtains deep rest; the mind is able to quiet itself as all aspects of one's being connect harmoniously with the universal energies. In this way one experiences and perceives subtle states of consciousness. Meditation allows negativity to surface and be dissolved. It also creates the space for intuitive, creative and inspirational insights.

Moving meditation is an essential aspect of self-cultivation. Such movement includes various exercises which develop the ability to guide one's internal and external energies. It is characterized by the "Eight Treasures" and "T'ai Chi movement." The Eight Treasures are a combination of breathing and energy guidance techniques which open the major channels of the body and allow the gathering of one's own energy and of the subtle energy in one's environment. They may be practiced independently or as a foundation for T'ai Chi movement. T'ai Chi movement induces the gathering, refinement and circulation of one's energy into more subtle channels. Such moving meditation integrates the body, mind and spirit, harmonizes one's internal energy with the universal law, and leads one to true health. It may be practiced by people of all ages.

Invocations are a technique for the guidance of subtle energy. They cause the response of the universal law. Through the practice of invocations, one may experientially prove the existence of the spiritual realms for oneself. Practiced diligently and consistently, they will restore one's mind and spirit to their original state of integrity and facilitate the ultimate realization of oneness with Tao.

An important part of the Integral Way of Life is the avoidance of excessive sexual activity. Achieved ones are not opposed to sexuality, but they are aware of possible negative influences of sexual activity. Excessiveness in sexual intercourse depletes one's vital energy and causes mental scatteredness and inefficiency. In determining the frequency of sexual activity, one needs to consider the natural rhythm of one's age and physical condition. According to the ancient energy calendar, there are certain days on which sexual intercourse violates the subtle energy of that particular time and may cause physical and mental disturbances. These specific days can be referred to on the ancient developed calendar. Dual cultivation also includes techniques which are taught by an achieved one at the appropriate time and on the appropriate level.

When practicing the Integral Way, one abstains from certain foods and substances such as raw or half-cooked meat, caffeine, strong spices, nicotine, narcotics and recreational drugs, prescription drugs, chemical food additives, improper herbs like peyote, etc., and strong alcoholic beverages.

The last basic aspect of disciplining oneself to one's own benefit is to abstain from unnecessary activities. Contemporary life is hectic. People spend much time and money in the pursuit of unnecessary "busy-ness." This is an unwise investment of one's life and energy. Eliminating activities which are not essential to one's life and well being allows more time for self-cultivation, quiet reflection or service to a worthwhile cause.

These eight aspects of integral truth are only the fundamental criteria of a healthy and balanced Way of life. If one is sincerely dedicated to one's personal development and spiritual evolution, it is best to seek the guidance and instruction of a true Master.

The Integral Way stresses not doing anything recklessly. One follows the natural Way and avoids violating the natural energy order. Universal law is not created by man but is naturally so. For example, every part of the human body has its own position and function. The vast universe also has an effective natural energy order just like the human body, and it will cause trouble if it is violated. The Integral Way is based on the plain reality of the universe and follows the direct way to restore a humans's true formless nature. Its teachings are concise and precise and cultivate the spirit itself.

Spiritual cultivation is composed of one's daily life activities, such as the way of speaking, the way of behaving, and all daily life movements. All of these are important elements of spiritual power development. They are the most elementary spiritual ceremonies. They restore spontaneity and deny any kind of mental manipulation. A natural human being is directed by his spiritual energy and causes appropriate responses not by need, but by pure spontaneity. Without design, one practices the very nature of the universe and connects oneself with universal simplicity. By simplifying one's activities, emotions, mind and spirit, one becomes united with the very essence of the universe. One conducts oneself exactly as a natural being. Then the universe responds not to one's manipulative mind, but to his or her pure spirit. When a human knows and embodies goodness, he or she receives good and beautiful responses. Through strict traditional spiritual training, one may become a completely developed human being.

> *Lieh Tzu had Lao Shang for his teacher and Po Kao Tzu for his friend. When he had fully mastered the systems of these two Taoists, he could ride home on the gentle breeze without difficulty. Yin Sheng heard of this and became his disciple. He dwelt with Lieh Tzu for many months without visiting his own home. While he was with him, he begged to be initiated into his secret arts. Ten times he asked and each time he received no answer. Becoming impatient, Yin Sheng announced his departure, but still Lieh Tzu gave no sign.*
>
> *So Yin Sheng went away, but after many months his mind was still unsettled and he returned to become*

his follower once more. Lieh Tzu said to him: "Why this incessant coming and going?" Yin Sheng replied: "Some time ago I sought instruction from you, Sir, but you would not tell me anything. That made me vexed with you, but now I have overcome that feeling and therefore I returned."

Lieh Tzu said: "Formerly I thought you were a man of penetration, have you fallen so low now? Sit down and I will tell you what I learned from my Master. After I had served Lao Shang and enjoyed the friend-ship of Po Kao Tzu for three years, my mind did not venture to reflect on right and wrong, and my lips did not venture to speak of profit and loss. Then for the first time, my Master bestowed one glance upon me - and that was all.

"At the end of five years a change had taken place; my mind was reflecting on right and wrong, and my lips were speaking of profit and loss. Then, for the first time, my Master relaxed his countenance and smiled. At the end of seven years there was another change. I let my mind reflect on what it would, but it no longer occupied itself with right and wrong. I let my lips utter whatsoever they pleased, but they no longer spoke of profit and loss. Then, at last, my Master led me in to sit on the mat beside him. At the end of nine years my mind gave free rein to its reflections and my mouth free passage to its speech. Of right and wrong, profit and loss, I had no knowledge neither as touching myself nor others. I knew neither that the Master was my teacher nor that the other man was my friend. Internal and external were blended into oneness. After that, there was no distinction between eye and ear, ear and nose, nose and mouth, all were the same.

"My mind was crystal clear, my body in dissolution, my flesh and bones all melted together. I was com-pletely unconscious of what my body was resting on, or what was under my feet. I was borne this way and that on the wind, like dry chaff or leaves falling from a tree. In fact, I knew not whether the wind was riding on me or I on the wind.

"Now, you have not spent one whole season in your teacher's house, and yet you have lost patience two or three times already. Why, at this rate the atmosphere will never support an atom of your body, and even the Earth will be unstable under the weight of one of your limbs!"

From this quotation of Lieh Tzu, an early Master of the Way, one may obtain insight into the Integral Way of Life.

The following "Observances for the Integral Way of Life" are guidelines to unite one's life with the Way.

First purify your heart by simplifying your mind and spirit. Thinking, speaking, doing and not doing all come forth from the origin of simplicity. To simplify the spirit is to achieve all else. Tao is elusive, but spiritual energy can become tangible through a sincere and true Way of thinking and acting. By seeing things only partially, we miss the target of complete uplifting of life. Diligently cultivate and deepen your roots in Tao. Deep roots in the eternal Tao are the foundation of immortality and freshness of spirit.

To be honest in self-cultivating and to make advancement step by step is the Way to achieve 'nonself' realization. Your spiritual evolution depends mainly on your daily self-inspection and self-examination. Stay on the right path and avoid self-destructive patterns. Avoid behavior which is harmful to yourself and to others. Mundane burdens obstruct our hearts and prevent success in the achievement of our spiritual actualization.

It takes three years to form a good habit, and only one day to destroy it. One moment of negligence can cause a lifetime of cultivation to deteriorate. Selfishness hardens the heart, while selflessness allows it to blossom. Unrighteous means will destroy good intentions. With pure energy one moves forward, with impure energy one digresses. In all matters, the eternal Tao is our final measure in choosing and

*determining our own life and behavior, both mentally
and practically.*

Daily Living

All of a person's daily movements and activities cause
responses from the subtle energy. Therefore it is important
to conduct oneself appropriately if one wants to achieve
harmony in one's life. Frequently occurring examples of
subtle energy response are those of telepathic nature. One
may think of something and open a book, and the same
topic will appear on that page. The same may happen with
the radio, television, or through a phone call. Speaking
about something can also influence its occurrence. Therefore one carefully chooses words and speaks only when
appropriate.

Another example is habits. If in the daytime one spends
much time in bed as if one were ill, then one will weaken
oneself and become prone to illness. These proofs occur in
ordinary situations of life and are projections of one's own
energy.

Achieved ones like to maintain the natural calmness of
the mind and in this way receive a clear and appropriate
energy response. Too much mental chatter weakens one's
mind and confuses the energy response. There are five
aspects of one's daily activities which need careful attention
and selection. These are one's thoughts, speech, company,
environment, and one's work or service to the world.

*The Yellow Emperor sat for fifteen years on the
throne and rejoiced that the Empire looked up to him
as its head. He was careful of his physical well-being,
sought pleasure for his ears and eyes, and gratified
his senses of taste and smell. Nevertheless, he grew
melancholy in spirit, his complexion became sallow,
and his sensations became dull and confused. Then
for another period of fifteen years he grieved that the
Empire was in disorder. He summoned all his intelligence and exhausted his resources of wisdom and
strength in trying to rule the people. In spite of it all,*

*his face remained haggard and pale, and his sensa-
tions dull and confused.*

*Then the Yellow Emperor sighed heavily and said:
"My fault is lack of moderation. This misery I suffer
comes from over-attention to my own self, and the troubles of the Empire from over-regulation of everything."
Thereupon he gave up all his schemes, abandoned his
ancestral palace, dismissed his attendants, removed
all the hanging bells, cut down the delicacies of his
cuisine, and returned to live at leisure in the private
apartments attached to the Court. There he fasted in
heart and, freeing himself from all his earthly desires,
he brought his body under natural control.*

*For many months he abstained from personal
intervention in government. Then he fell asleep in the
daytime. He had a vision that he made a journey to
the Kingdom of Hua-hsu, the Realm of Absolute Being,
situated many tens of thousands of miles from the
state of Ch'i. It was beyond the reach of ship or
vehicle or any mortal foot. Only the soul could travel
so far.*

*This kingdom trusted the nature of the universe as
its head or ruler and it simply went of itself. Its people
were without desires or cravings and simply followed
their natural instincts. They felt neither joy in life nor
abhorrence of death, thus they came to no untimely
ends. They felt neither attachment to self nor indiffer-
ence to others, thus they were exempt from love and
hatred alike. They knew neither aversion from one
course nor inclination to another, hence profit and loss
existed not among them. All were equally untouched
by the emotions of love and sympathy or of jealousy
and fear. Water had no power to drown them, fire
could not burn them, cuts and blows caused them
neither injury nor pain, scratching or tickling could not
make them itch. They bestrode the air as though
treading on solid earth and they were cradled in space
as though resting in a bed. Clouds and mist obstruct-
ed not their vision, peals of thunder could not stun
their ears, physical beauty disturbed not their hearts,*

> *mountains and valleys hindered not their steps. They*
> *moved about like absolute beings.*
> *When the Yellow Emperor returned from his vision,*
> *he summoned his three highest Ministers and told*
> *them what he had seen. "For many months," he said,*
> *"I have been living a life of leisure, fasting in heart,*
> *subduing my body, and casting about in my mind for*
> *the true Way of nourishing my own life and regulating*
> *the lives of others. Yet I failed to discover the secret.*
> *Worn out, I fell asleep and had this vision. Now I*
> *know that the Way is not to be sought through the*
> *senses. This Way I know and hold within me, yet I*
> *cannot impart it to you."*
> *For twenty-eight years after this, there was great*
> *order in the Empire. It nearly equalled the state of the*
> *Kingdom of Hua-hsu, the Realm of Absolute Being.*
> *After the Emperor ascended on high to Heaven, the*
> *absolute realm, the people bewailed him for two*
> *hundred years without intermission.*

The Yellow Emperor reigned for two hundred years and became an example of the Integral Way of Life. In later generations this Way was called Huang-Lao, as an abbreviation for Huang Ti (or Yellow Emperor) and Lao Tzu. However, these achieved ones only continued the Way of life transmitted to them through Fu Shi and Shen Nung and many other ancient sages. The origin of the Integral Way dates back to the plain and unknown people who lived this natural Way of life before written history began.

The Sacred Method
Another area which uses the principle of energy response is the practice of spiritual methods, referred to in the Integral Way as the Sacred Method or the Divine Way. This involves the performance of miracles in the context of ordinary life and the utilization of specific methods to cause specific responses from the subtle energy. There are some misguided people who use certain methods in order to do evil, generally referred to as black magic. Those who practice

black magic not only do damage to others, but also cause their own destruction in response to their actions. The Sacred Method of causing a response of the divine energy of the universe brings blessing to the lives of others as well as to one's own life. Through this strict and precise method of developing spiritual energy one may connect one's energy with the spiritual realm.

Achieved ones perform spiritual miracles in daily life. Life itself is magical and miraculous. A practitioner of the Integral Way considers things like "bad luck" or "bad dreams" mere dramatic effects in his miraculous life. The purification and sublimation of his or her energy are the daily practices of an achieved one. However, divine measures can be used only for divine purposes. To use spiritual methods as a profession for the purpose of making money or increasing one's reputation will diminish one's character and energy. On the other hand, to subtly and inconspicuously use them to help people or further one's own spiritual growth will enhance one's energy. Some invocations and talismans are used to ally oneself with a natural energy. Some are for awakening one's deep subtle energy or refining one's gross energy to the subtle level. To extend one's spiritual blessing to the world is the highest magic performed in daily life.

> *Chao Hsiang Tzu led a company of a hundred thousand men out to hunt in the Central Mountains. Lighting the dry undergrowth, they set fire to the whole forest, and the glow of flames was visible for a hundred miles around. Suddenly a man appeared, emerging from a rocky cliff, and was seen hovering in the air amidst the flames and the smoke. Everybody took him for a disembodied spirit. When the fire had passed, he walked quietly out and showed no trace of having been through the ordeal.*
>
> *Chao Hsiang Tzu marveled thereat and detained the man for careful examination. In bodily form he was undoubtedly a man, possessing the seven channels of sense, besides which his breathing and voice*

also proclaimed him to be a man. The Prince inquired what secret power enabled him to dwell in rock and walk through fire. "Exactly what do you mean by rock?" replied the man; "and what do you mean by fire?"

Chao Hsiang Tzu said: "What you just now came out of is rock and what you just now walked through is fire."

"I know nothing of them," replied the man.

The incident reached the ears of the Marquis Wen of the Wei state, who spoke to Chao Hsiang Tzu about it, saying: "What an extraordinary man that must be!"

"From what I have heard the Master say," replied Chao Hsiang Tzu, "the man who achieves harmony with Tao enters into close unison with external objects, and none of them have the power to harm or hinder him. Passing through solid metal or stone, walking in the midst of fire or on the surface of water, all these things become possible to him."

"Why, my friend," asked the Marquis, "Can you not do all this?"

"I have not yet succeeded," said Chao Hsiang Tzu, "in cleansing my heart of impurities and in discarding wisdom. I can only find leisure to discuss the matter in tentative fashion."

"And why," pursued the Marquis, "does the Master himself not perform all these miracles?"

"The Master," replied Chao Hsiang Tzu, "is able to do these things, but he is also able to refrain from doing them." This answer highly enlightened and delighted the Marquis.

This anecdote is another valuable teaching of Lieh Tzu.

Lao Ch'eng Tzu went to learn spiritual methods from the venerable Yin Wei. After a period of three years, having obtained no communication, he humbly asked permission to go home. Yin Wen bowed and led him into the inner apartment. There, having dismissed his attendants, he spoke to him as follows: "Long ago,

when Lao Tzu was setting out on his journey to the
West, he addressed me and said: 'All that has the
breath of life, all that possesses bodily form, is mere
illusion. The point at which creation begins and the
change effected by the dual principle are called life
and death respectively. That which underlies the
manifold workings of destiny is called evolution; that
which produces and transforms bodily substance is
called illusion. The ingenuity of the creative power is
mysterious and its operations are profound. In truth,
it is inexhaustible and eternal. The ingenuity of the
subtle source which causes material form is patent to
the eye and its operations are not superficial. There-
fore it arises immediately and immediately it vanish-
es.' Only one who knows that life is really illusion and
that death is really evolution can begin to learn spiritu-
al methods from me. You and I are both illusions.
What need, then, to make a study of the subject?"

Lao Ch'eng Tzu returned home, and for many
months pondered deeply over the words of the venera-
ble Yin Wei. Subsequently he had the power of
appearing or disappearing at will; he could reverse the
order of the four seasons, produce thunderstorms in
winter and ice in summer, make flying things creep
and creeping things fly. Yet to the end of his days he
never revealed the secret of his art. (Lieh Tzu)

Praying

Prayer is the communication of one's needs or desires to a
higher power such as to God or a particular name. Through
prayer one may cause the response of the subtle energy. All
religions stress communication between human beings and
their concept of a divine sovereign. Prayer, whether embel-
lished or simple, is generally the vehicle through which this
communication is transmitted. Despite the fact that most
people use prayer primarily as an emotional release, it is
beyond doubt that a sincere and consistent prayer will
cause a subtle energy response. However, one must be

unemotional and have a disciplined mind in order to cause an appropriate response.

Different cultures and traditions emphasize particular names of images as the objects of their prayers. In fact, people may direct their prayers to any object and they may still receive a response. In ancient China, for example, people would pray to a well or the "water" energy; the kitchen stove or the "fire" energy; to very old trees or the "wood" energy; to high mountains or the "earth" energy; or to ancient swords and weapons, the "metal" energy, and they would receive a response through their sincerity. The response is also influenced by the energy of the person who uses the objects toward which the prayer is directed. In some parts of India there are temples dedicated to rats and snakes, and prayers to these spirits have also caused responses. People who have prayed to an empty house or room have received an energy response through their own soul power, just as they have through praying to anything else.

The truth is that the responsive subtle energy is everywhere in the universe and also within the person who prays. The response will be positive if the subtle energy waves are projected properly. The responsive energy is not bound by images or names which may become obstacles to direct communication with it. Yet, because the frequency of the projected vibration is an essential factor, the vibration created by the use of the correct name of an energy is the real secret of spiritual traditions. However, when people adopt names out of their ignorance of spiritual truth, they hinder the liberation of their souls.

The phenomenon of energy response may be explained in two ways. One would be to say that the objects are powerful enough to assist the minds of the praying people in the performance of these miracles. The other way would be to say that the corresponding phase of energy evolution responds to the cause of the prayer. The truth is that human nature and the nature of the universe are one and the same. There is no distinction between individual energy and universal energy.

The teachings of the Integral Way uses specific invocations which are designed to create effective and appropriate responses. The following invocation is addressed to the "Jade Emperor," which is the directing energy of the multi-universe. It is called "Daily Communion with the Jade Emperor" and is practiced for spiritual centering.

In the vastness of the universe
*   there are many heavenly realms.*
In the center of each
*   resides its own Jade Emperor,*
*   the universal Master.*
While appearing as many,
*   in substance all Jade Emperors are one.*
The 'Undecayed One' is his divine title.
His true name is 'Self-So.'
The universe is his body
*   and cosmic law his uniting principle.*
He is the mind of the known
*   and the eye of the unknown.*
The giving and taking of life
*   are his self-expression*
*   and the exercise of his eternality.*

People are his spiritual offspring
*   and the heavenly born nobility.*
Because they are self-corrupting
*   they lose their pristine high qualities.*
The Jade Emperor reestablishes himself in humankind
*   as a still and flexible mind.*
The self-commanded and easy mind
*   is the government of the Jade Emperor in man.*
The only command he gives to his moral descendants
*   is to live in harmony with the natural cosmic order.*

He educates them with self-knowledge,
   and self-refinement is the venerable rank
   he confers to them.
He bestows his blessings
   upon those of self-cultivation.
Self-contentment is the reward
   he gives to his divine lineage.
To those of high self-awareness
   his heavenly assignment
   is the realization of their divine nature.
He fulfills the one who has self-dignity
   and establishes the one who renounces himself.
He subdues no one as he regulates the universe.
He favors those who help themselves
   and hinders those who are slothful and inert.
He gives energy to those who have positive virtue
   and takes it away from those who have self-doubt.
Self-contradiction is the punishment
   he gives to the vulgar-minded.
He brings calamity to the overly self-concerned
   and delivers tragedy to the self-indulgent.
Shock and misfortune are his warnings
   to those who are self-deceived.
He shackles those who have self-pity
   and blinds the opinionated.
He chains the self-centered
   and penalizes excessive self-love and self-hate.
Simplicity is his great teaching
   and harmony his abiding principle.
Egolessness is his key
   for the attainment of greatness.
Selflessness is his secret
   for the achievement of immortality.
He is most supreme
   because he is self-forgetting.
The clarity and purity of his being
   is the source of all fulfillment.
He is the unruling ruler of all life.

Another invocation for general use is the "Daily Mental Discipline":

I am the offspring
     of the divine nature of the universe.
Through the extension of the positive, creative
     and constructive nature of the universe,
     I have received life.
Let pure, positive energy display itself
     in my nature and daily life.
Let only the highest energy
     be exhibited in my speech and behavior.
In my relationships with my fellow men and women,
     let me demonstrate the benevolence
     of the universal nature.

Let pure, positive energy
     be the only experience of my being.
Let my spirit and mind be a reflection
     of the sublime order and harmony of the universe,
     and my body an expression of the Subtle Origin.
When eating, let the pure and positive nature
     nourish me directly.
When sleeping, let the peaceful nature refresh me.
When working, let the divine nature
     be expressed through me.
Let my life follow the Way of universal nature.

Let my life be the realization
     of the divine nature of the universe.
So that I can be the positive manifestation
     of the Subtle Origin
     and unite myself firmly
     with the incorruptible spirit,
     the Jade Emperor,
     the supreme core of the universe.

Contemporary and even some ancient scholars usually doubt that energy response actually occurs. When the mind is trapped within the confines of form, it is impossible to recognize the essence of creation. As ancient Master Lieh Tzu says:

> There may be similarity in understanding without similarity in outward form. There may also be similarity in outward form without similarity in understanding. The sage embraces similarity of understanding and pays no regard to similarity in form. The world in general is attracted by similarity of form, but remains indifferent to similarity of understanding. The creatures that resemble them in shape they love and consort with; those that differ from them in shape they fear and keep at a distance.
> The creature that has hands shaped differently from its feet, hair on its head and an even set of teeth in its jaws, and walks erect, is called man. Yet it does not follow that a man may not have the mind of a brute. Even though this may be the case, other men will still recognize him as one of their own species by virtue of his outward form. Creatures that have wings on their back or horns on their head, serrated teeth or extensile talons, that fly overhead or run on all fours, are called birds and beasts. Yet it does not follow that a bird or a beast may not have the mind of a man. Yet, even if this be so, it is nevertheless assigned to another species because of the difference in form.

Highly achieved ones generally do not engage in prayer. They spontaneously respond to the true nature of their lives. They praise their simple lives rather than ask for favors through prayers. The events of their lives are always spontaneous and occur beautifully and smoothly without their own design. In worldly life, however, there are many occasions when it is appropriate to use the subtle power of prayer. Prayer is one way to compose one's mental energy to evoke a response from the subtle realm of the universe.

One may use a prayer in one's own life and also to help others.

According to the principle of energy response, any simple prayer, if applied properly, will cause the appropriate response. When following the Integral Way of Life one has an even mind and respect for the true nature of all beings and things. One is protected by one's even-mindedness and one's harmony with the universal nature causes harmonious responses in one's life.

Reverent Offerings

One should cultivate the habit or mental attitude of having respect and reverence for the subtle realm, for this is the first important requirement which may cause the response of subtle energy. One may direct one's offering to the subtle energy of the universe as manifested in spiritual beings and spiritually illuminated people. The token of one's offering may be flowers, which symbolize the freshness of one's mind and spirit; fruit, which symbolizes the abundance of one's life; clean foods, money or one's own creative energy in the form of service to the spiritual realm. Do not offer meat or shed the blood of animals as an offering or thanksgiving. Also, offering food or drink to one's concept of God is of no value if one is attempting to bribe the supposed external sovereign in order to obtain blessings. Appreciate the sacredness of spirit and perform all activities of life in a centered way, in quietude and with reverence.

To offer every moment of life in veneration and gratitude is the highest offering a person can make. In this way a person enhances awareness of and connection with the subtle reality of one's being. Making an offering without asking for something in return is much more beneficial and important than making a prayer that involves a request, because the offering is a personal manifestation of respect and benevolence. Merely asking the spiritual realm for favors in the form of prayers erroneously puts one in the position of spiritual inferiority.

How does the spiritual realm interact with one's offering? There is no other person to accept what is offered and to give something back as a reward. Spiritual rituals concern the harmonization of one's own energy with the subtle energy. Offerings are the manifestation of a person's own nature, and with the qualities of respect, generosity and benevolence, one manifests the same response in life. This fact seems to be the highest secret to those who are spiritually blind. By engaging in the spiritual ritual of reverent offering, a person will enjoy greater abundance in life than through spending time asking and searching for satisfaction. The highest offering is the performance of every activity in every aspect of life with respect and reverence. The true practice of the Integral Way is the offering of one's pure spirit in all daily occasions.

The creative energy of Heaven
    is the paternal source of our being.
The receptive energy of Earth
    is the maternal source of our being.
Receptive and creative energies combine
    to give birth
    to all beings and potential beings.
Tao is the true origin of all life.
Heaven, Earth and Tao
    dwell in all humanity.
Thus, the way to serve Heaven, Earth and Tao
    is to serve one's fellow men and women.
In Tao, we have life as well as life's virtues.
Living in a temple or church
    does not necessarily mean
    that a person is spiritual or virtuous.
Temples, churches and statues
    are mere symbols and images.
An achieved one is not misled by external appearances,
    but instead focuses on the true,
    inner spiritual source.

The worship of force and the suggestion of conquest
  is the way of worldly religions
  and modern civilizations.
The worldly point of view states
  that might is right.
According to the Universal Integral Way,
  righteousness is might.
Subtlety and gentleness are the Way
  of cultivating eternity in the spiritual tradition.
When we worship, we do not distinguish
  between the internal and external,
  or indulge in the creation of spectacular visions.
With gentleness, we always maintain
  the spirit of creativity.
When the creative spirit sings in our hearts,
  our surroundings benefit
  from the compassion we radiate.
We use gentle means to educate people
  and nurture their spiritual growth.
We care not for profit, but are interested only
  in serving the eternal Tao.

Good Deeds

> *There was once a man, a sailor by profession, who was fond of sea gulls. Every morning he went into the ocean and swam about in their midst, at which times a hundred gulls and more would constantly flock about him. One day his father said to him: "I am told that the sea gulls swim about you in the water. I wish you would catch one or two for me to make pets of them." On the following day the sailor went to the ocean as usual. But lo! The gulls only wheeled about in the air and would not alight.* (Lieh Tzu)

If the energy embodied by man is harmonious it will naturally express itself as benevolence toward all creation, and in response he will be treated with benevolence by all other beings and things. There is no need to create special occasions for being benevolent. The subtle energy responds most effectively when one's expression is spontaneous and within the course of ordinary life. Being benevolent only toward a particular person or motivated by one's own particular preference will be futile. The attempt to appease one's troubled conscience through charities will cause a negative response of subtle energy. According to the unfailing principle of subtle energy response, it is impossible to be hypocritical before the universal law.

Benevolence displays itself inconspicuously, naturally and spontaneously, and causes positive and constructive responses. When a person is living and acting benevolently, his or her life will be a reflection of the inner harmonious energy.

> In the course of Lieh Tzu's instruction by Hu-Ch'iu Tzu-Lin, the latter said to him: "You must familiarize yourself with the universal law of subtle energy response before you can speak of regulating conduct."
>
> Lieh Tzu said: "Will you explain what you mean by the universal law of subtle energy response?"
>
> "Look at your shadow," said the Master, "and then you will know." Lieh Tzu turned and looked at his shadow. When his body was bent, the shadow was bent; when his body was straight, the shadow was straight. Thus it appeared that the attributes of being bent or straight were not inherent in the shadow, but corresponded to certain positions of the body. Likewise, contraction and extension are not inherent in the subject, but occur in correspondence to external causes. The universal law of subtle energy response follows the same principle.
>
> Kuan Yin spoke to Master Lieh Tzu, saying: "If speech is sweet the echo will be sweet; if speech is harsh the echo will be harsh. If the body is long the shadow will be long; if the body is short the shadow will be short. Reputation is like the echo, personal experiences are like the shadow. Hence the saying: 'Heed your words and they will meet with harmonious

*response; heed your actions and they will find agree-
able accord.' Therefore the sage observes the origin in
order to know the issue, scrutinizes the past in order
to know the future. Such is the principle whereby he
attains foreknowledge."*

*The standard of conduct lies within one's own self;
the testing of it lies with other men. We are impelled
to love those who love us and to hate those who hate
us. T'ang and Wu loved the Empire and therefore
each became King. Chieh and Chou hated the Empire
and therefore they perished. Here we have the test
applied. He who does not follow Tao when standard
and test are both clear, may be likened to the one who
when leaving a house does not go by the door or when
travelling abroad does not keep to the straight road.
To gain profit in this way is surely impossible.*

When living in the relative realm, one may practice good
deeds in order to further one's development toward natural
benevolence. There are two kinds of good deeds. One is referred to as yang or apparent good deeds, in which every-
body is aware of the fact that one has done something good;
the other is yin or hidden good deeds, in which no one
knows that one has done something good. With yang good
deeds, the person benefits in that he receives recognition
and social prestige. However, this kind of activity is valuable only in the relative realm and can actually hinder one's
spiritual development. Yin good deeds do not seek a reward
or recognition from anyone. The practice of yin good deeds
deeply enhances one's spirit and is called absolute behavior.
The following are ten guidelines for enhancing the Spirit of
Life:

1. *Sincerely follow Tao, the path to eternal life. To turn
   one's back to the Subtle Origin is to face darkness and
   degeneration of the soul.*

2. *Experience and cherish the pure happiness within your
   own soul. It is eternal and constant. The treasures of*

the world are deceptive and fleeting, causing the progressive erosion of one's subtle, spiritual essence.

3. Be plain, simple, honest and practical when dealing with
the world. It is better to be naive than cunning. Better
to be fooled than suspicious.

4. Consider righteousness before profit. To gain profit and
lose virtue is no bargain.

5. Pay attention to the laws of the world. Behave with
conscience and maintain dignity. In this way you
protect the freedom for self-cultivation.

6. Plant yourself firmly in Tao. As the tide ebbs and flows,
so does the great transformation of the ten thousand
things sweep away all but the firmly rooted.

7. Become familiar with the law of cause and effect, and
deeply penetrate the truth of the universal law of subtle
energy response. To sow is to reap. Energies of the
same frequency attract each other. Therefore, blind
desires lead to blind alleys and righteousness leads to
eternality.

8. Share happiness with others. By extending ourselves to
others we enlarge our being. Selfless service is our
sacred vow. Receiving by giving is the universal law of
supply.

9. Unite yourself with Heaven and Earth. Be unconcerned
with life and death. With clarity and self-awareness
developed through self-cultivation transform your being,
and thus end your bondage to the law of the great
transformation.

10. Clearly and completely discern the heart of the un-
adorned teachings. Passed down through generations,

*they have come from our ancient Masters. Our Way is
the gathering of the greatest simple truths. The well-
spring of eternal life is the infinite simplicity of Tao.*

Dreaming

Some people are able to cause a response of the subtle
energy through their dreams, and others are not; some
dreams cause response, while others do not. The response
may be on the physical or on the spiritual level. Dreams are
more subtle and therefore more difficult to control than
daytime behavior.

There are two categories of dreams. One type of dream
is caused by messages from within the body. As one's
energy circulates through the body it passes by and stimu-
lates the nerves of different parts of the body which will
transmit messages to the brain. In other words, the energy
tells stories about the real feelings and images of body and
mind in the form of a mental stage play. The different
spheres and parts of the body through which the energy
flows will cause the brain to be stimulated in various areas,
creating distinct impressions in one's consciousness.

The other type of dream is caused by messages received
from outside the body. These dreams may be rehearsal of
an event that will happen in the future, the telepathic
message that something is happening thousands of miles
away, or a communication from another being. This type of
dream happens when one's own subtle energy connects with
the subtle energy of an event or another being.

Usually, highly evolved people have no dreams because
they have few desires. The peaceful mind sleeps lightly.
The reality of one's life is the reality of one's mind. The most
useful and valid dreams occur when one's energy is connected clearly, straightly and directly with one's internal or
with external energies. Then the message to one's consciousness will also be straight and clear. If one cultivates
one's energy well, then one will be able to guide one' dreams
and use them advantageously.

Master Lieh Tzu said,

*A dream is an energy that comes into contact with
the mind; an external event is an energy that impinges
on the body. Hence our feelings by day and our
dreams by night are the result of contacts made by
body and mind. It follows that if one can concentrate
one's mind in abstraction, one's feelings and dreams
will vanish by themselves. Those who rely on their
waking perceptions will argue about them. Those who
put faith in dreams do not understand the processes
of change in the internal and external energy cycles.
"The pure men of old passed their waking existence in
self-oblivion and slept without dreams." How can this
be dismissed as an empty phrase?*

The following invocation may be used to cleanse the
unpleasant or frightening shadow remaining from the
experience of a bad dream and to prevent its occurrence in
the physical reality of life; it must be practiced diligently and
properly. It is called the "Purification from Heaven and
Earth."

*Heaven and Earth are spontaneous manifestations
        of the wondrous, universal law.
As the original oneness expresses itself
        gross and subtle energy become distinctly divided.
My "Bodily Cave" is brightly illuminated
        by the mysterious light from the three sources,
        my three tan tien.*

*The powerful spirits of the eight directions
        conjoin my being with the true origin of life.
By the absolute order of the divine Ling Pao[1]
        in the highest Ninth Heaven,
        send the positive energy of Chien Luo, Tan Na,*

---

[1]The heavenly reverent spiritual authority.

> *Dan Kan and Tai Shuan*[2] *to destroy my spiritual*
> *obstacles and debilitate any evil influences.*
> For this divine invocation
> *is given to the highest sovereignty.*
> It is a jade oracle from the Subtle Origin.
> I read this invocation with strong sincerity
> *to drive away the demons and evils*
> *in order to lengthen my years.*
> With this order, the attained spirits respond to me.
> *The evil demon king, Mu Wang, is chained to stand*
> *as my guard and servant.*
> *The negative atmosphere has been cleansed.*
> *The chi of Tao is everlasting.*
> *So it is commanded.*

Divination

Divination is the practice of foretelling the future or discovering the unknown. The sages of ancient China developed systems for divination which are the most precise, most effective and most developed methods for obtaining correct answers to questions and to foretell the future. The art of mystical prediction is based on the universal law of energy response.

The most famous and elementary of these systems is the renowned *I Ching* or *Book of Changes and the Unchanging Truth* which originated as a spiritual science in prehistoric times and has only relatively recently been introduced to the western world. It involves the use of coins or Chinese yarrow sticks, or any other suggestive method, to gain insight into the energy arrangement of a particular thing or event. The ancient developed ones also developed other very accurate and more mystical divination methods like "The Gate of Mystery and the Hidden Jya," "The Highest Wisdom of the Six Heavenly Yang Water Energies" and "The Greatest

---

[2]These are the most powerful energies in nature and are named as spiritual guardians.

Yi Governing All Wonders," which surpass the system of the *I Ching* by giving information on may specific details.

There are hundreds of divination methods which work on different levels and are for specific purposes. All are effective and have their own special way for answering questions. Evidence gathered through countless generations verifies that the subtle spiritual energy formed by the person practicing divination can cause the response of the universal energy which will give the appropriate answer through the divination method. One may also say that the images have already taken form in the diviner's mind and the external system merely develops the picture for the purpose of correct judgement.

These techniques for answering questions and finding solutions are just as accurate in the realm of mind and spirit as is the scientific method in the physical realm. Obviously the coins, sticks or any other tools work only to reveal the answer to one's question. They are extensions of the mind which vibrate the subtle energy network and receive the answer through the principle of energy response.

The hidden value of all spiritual divination systems is more profound than the mere ability to determine what will happen in the future. These systems train the mind to achieve a very high level of sensitivity, and ultimately, even without practicing a divination method one will be in direct contact with the subtle realm and have intuitive knowledge of everything.

Some divination systems demonstrate and expound the principle of interaction between the yin and yang energies which govern all events and relationships in the universe. Through the principles of yin and yang and the five phases of energy evolution one can reveal all unknown events and facts. If one retraces the development of the multi-universe one can reach the ultimate reality, the realm of all existence and non-existence. One can return from the multiplicity of universal appearances to the undivided oneness of Tao.

Master Lieh Tzu says:

The inspired ones of old regarded yin and yang as controlling both Heaven and Earth. But that which has substance is engendered from that which is devoid of substance. Out of what then were Heaven and Earth engendered?

There is a creative principle which is itself uncreated; there is a principle of change which is itself unchanging. The uncreated is able to create life; the unchanging is able to effect change. That which is produced cannot but continue producing; that which is evolved cannot but continue evolving. Hence there is constant production and constant evolution. The law of constant production and evolution at no time ceases to operate. The uncreated we may surmise to be alone in itself. The unchanging goes to and fro, and its range is illimitable. We may surmise that it stands alone, and that its ways are inexhaustible.

Hence we say, there is a great principle of change, a great origin, a great beginning and a great primordial simplicity. In the great change, substance is not yet manifest. In the great origin lies the beginning of substance. In the great beginning lies the beginning of material form. In the great simplicity lies the beginning of essential qualities.

When substance, form and essential qualities are still blended together it is called the undivided oneness. Undivided oneness means that all things are organically interlaced and not yet separated from one another. The purer and lighter elements, tending upwards, made the Heavens; the grosser and heavier elements, tending downwards, made the Earth. Substance, harmoniously proportioned became man; and Heaven and Earth thus containing a spiritual element produced and evolved all things.

Geomancy

The integral science of geomancy is the knowledge of the location of subtle energy rays in the physical universe and their relation to human life. The fundamental knowledge of geomancy is simple and was developed through the intuitive ability of humans. A person with a highly developed sensitivity has a nervous system which informs one of the subtle energies present in a certain location or situation, and he or she will thus become alert to unfavorable and dangerous energies.

The subtle factors of a person's life vary depending on the angle and direction of the subtle energy rays one is exposed to and connected with. Subtle energy radiations influence one's marriage, health, financial situation and all other aspects of life. This influence is effective when one harmonizes with the subtle energy as well as when one violates it.

By applying the knowledge of geomancy, an individual may skillfully proceed with one's life and choose the appropriate and favorable times and locations to engage in business activities or to establish a residence. The Integral Way has the knowledge of how to draw physical, mental and spiritual sustenance from the inexhaustible treasure of Tao.

> *Mr. Kuo of the state of Ch'i was very rich, while Mr. Hsiang of the state of Sung was very poor. The latter travelled from Sung to Ch'i and asked the other for the secret of his prosperity. Mr. Kuo told him: "It is because I am a good thief," he said. "The first year I began to be a thief I had just enough. The second year I had ample. The third year I reaped a great harvest. And in the course of time I found myself the owner of whole villages and districts."*
>
> *Mr. Hsiang was overjoyed; he understood the word "thief" in its literal sense, but he did not understand the true way of becoming a thief. Accordingly, he climbed over walls and broke into houses, grabbing everything he could see and lay hands upon. But before long his thefts brought him trouble and he was stripped even of what he had previously possessed. Thinking that Mr. Kuo had basely deceived him, Mr. Hsiang went to him with a bitter complaint. "Tell me," said Mr. Kuo, "how did you set about being a thief?"*

On learning from Mr. Hsiang what had happened he cried out, "Alas and alack! You have been brought to this pass because you went to work the wrong way. Now let me put you on the right track. We all know that Heaven has its seasons and that the earth has its riches. Well, the things that I steal are the riches of Heaven and Earth, each in their season, the fertilizing rain water from the clouds and the natural products of mountain and meadow land.

"Thus I grow my grain and ripen my crops, build my walls and construct my tenements. From the dry land I steal winged and four-footed game, from the rivers I steal fish and turtles. There is nothing that I do not steal. For corn and grain, clay and wood, bird and beasts, fish and turtles are all creations of nature. How can I claim them as mine? Yet, stealing in this way from nature I bring no retribution upon myself. But gold, jade and precious stones, stores of grain, silk stuffs and other kinds of property are things accumulated by men, not bestowed upon us by nature. So who can complain if he gets into trouble stealing them?"

Mr. Hsiang, in a state of great perplexity and fearing to be led astray a second time by Mr. Kuo, went off to consult Tung Kuo, a man of learning. Tung Kuo said to him, "Are you not already a thief in respect to your own body? You are stealing the harmony of yin and yang in order to keep alive and to maintain your bodily form. How much more then are you a thief with regard to external possessions! Heaven and Earth cannot be dissociated from the myriad objects of nature. To claim any one of these as your own betokens confusion of thought. Mr. Kuo's thefts are carried out in a spirit of justice and therefore bring no retribution. But your thefts were carried out in a spirit of selfishness and therefore they brought you troubles. Those who take possession of property whether public or private are thieves."

The discovery and the utilization of the subtle energy in the universe is a treasure which is accessible to everyone. If one is equipped with knowledge and special techniques, one can make use of the subtle energy just as one uses the physical power inherent in air, water, sunshine and mineral wealth, in the form of, for example, coal, oil and gas, or wind, electrical, solar and atomic power. The bountiful resources of nature belong to no one. Thus master Lieh Tzu referred to all who claim and use the creations of nature as clever "thieves."

Chapter 10

Mystical Changes
in Achieved People
of the Integral Way

Connecting One's Personal Energy with the Subtle, Divine Energy of the Universe

When the mind is rectified, the body reflects its balance. Old physical maladies gradually and completely disappear. One is no longer tempted by former bad habits, nor does one chase after worldly pleasures. One stands firmly on one's own two feet. Deep calm pervades one's internal and external atmosphere. One has both the time and the energy to accomplish any task. One purifies oneself and is at peace with one's environment. One never becomes violent and has untiring patience with one's fellow beings. One is free of worry and always has a joyful heart.

One is never jealous of another's pre-eminence, and never greedy for possessions prized by others. One has no ambition to live a vain or luxurious life. Because one lives simply, one maintains serenity. One keeps one's physical desire subdued and one's virtues high. One develops true and deep self-knowledge, dissolves all obstacles, and extends oneself to meet the straight and eternal Way. Thus, one experiences uncritically that all concepts of life and death are merely the ebb and flow of the eternal breath of Tao.

One dissolves one's ego and with it all conflicts between internal and external. One does not seek one's own longevity or personal happiness, nor does one struggle to hold on to material things. One does not use the speakable as truth to suppress those who are silent. One has no desire to go beyond one's means or ability. In one's pure mind, there are no illusions or strange thinking. One nurtures a firm character through selfless giving and self-oblivion. One never emphasizes that one's actions are right, nor does one claim credit for one's undertakings.

One knows things thoroughly from beginning to end. Virtuously, one knows there are certain things one will never do. One avoids involvement in contests for worldly profit or glory. One is amiable and useful. One embodies harmonious equilibrium and creative appropriateness. One enjoys ease both internally and externally. One strives only to surpass one's own virtues. One obeys the universal spirit in order to evolve higher. Before touching the formed, one rests in the unformed. One enlightens oneself and never tires of awakening the world.

When Master Lieh Tzu took up his abode in Nan-kuo the number of those who settled with him was past reckoning even if one were to count them day by day. Lieh Tzu, however, continued to live in retirement, and every morning would hold discussions with them, the fame of which spread far and wide.

Kan-kuo Tzu was his next door neighbor, but for twenty years no visit passed between them, and when they met in the street they acted as though they had not seen each other. Lieh Tzu's disciples felt convinced that there was enmity between their Master and Kan-kuo Tzu; and at last, one who had come from the State of Ch'u spoke to Lieh Tzu about it, saying, "How is it, Sir, that you and Kan-Kuo Tzu are enemies?"

"Kan-Kuo Tzu," he replied, "has the appearance of fullness, but his mind is blank. His ears do not hear, his eyes do not see, his mouth does not speak, his mind is devoid of knowledge and his body free from agitation. What would be the object of visiting him? We will try, however, and you shall accompany me there to see for yourselves."

Accordingly, forty of the disciples went with him to call on Kan-kuo Tzu, who turned out to be a repulsive-looking creature with whom they could make no contact. He only gazed blankly at Lieh Tzu. His mind and body seemed not to belong together, and his guests could find no means of approach. Suddenly,

Kan-kuo Tzu singled out the hindmost row of Lieh Tzu's disciples, and began to talk to them quite pleasantly and simply, though in the tone of a superior. The disciples were astonished at this, and when they got home again, all wore a puzzled expression.

Master Lieh Tzu said, "He who has attained perfect knowledge is silent. He who uses silence in lieu of speech really does speak. He who for knowledge substitutes blankness of mind really does know. Without words and speaking not, he really speaks and really knows. Saying nothing and knowing nothing, there is in reality nothing that he does not say, and nothing he does not know. This is how the matter stands, and there is nothing further to be said. Why are you thus astonished without cause?"

Conclusion

The entire universe is but the manifestation of energy. When the vibration of this energy is gross and heavy, it becomes tangible and perceivable by the five senses of human beings. We call this physical energy or the material plane. When the vibration is subtle and light, it becomes invisible, intangible to the five physical senses and is called subtle energy or the spiritual plane. These are the two categories of universal manifestation, the yin and the yang. The ancient achieved ones called the integration of yin and yang the T'ai Chi - the ultimate law of the universe. The entity of the individualized human being embodies both physical and spiritual energy, evolving and developing mental energy in the post-natal stage of life. Thus, a human may be considered a small model of the universe. The vast universe is a T'ai Chi and the individual human being is also a T'ai Chi.

The world's leaders hold the view that human survival is the result of struggle, conquest and confrontation. According to the integral view, however, man's survival is ensured by the reintegration of yin and yang energies. The harmonization of opposite forces at all times is the only way to assure man's survival. Surely, the phenomena of contention, struggle and conquest exist as minor and partial factors in the whole process of harmonization of the living sphere of human societies, in the long-lasting human history, and in the entire universal evolution. The belief that tensions, conflicts and wars are necessary and unavoidable is widespread. Yet if one calmly looks back and reviews the whole of human history, whether eastern or western, local or international, contemporary or ancient, it is not difficult to recognize and understand that unhealthy tensions and wars were, are, and will be, unnecessary and a waste of human life.

Once I tried to tell this to a friend who was engaged in some kind of fighting. He responded impatiently and said: "If you and someone else fall into the sea, and both of you do not know how to swim and there is only one plank, enough to ensure the survival of only one person, Master Ni, do you fight for it or do you die?" This is a supposed situation. My friend had a chance to look at his real life situation again differently and the fight did not occur. Obviously my friend and the other person, his apparent enemy, did not "drown in the sea."

I hope that all humanity may come to know that most of the tensions and conflicting situations in human life, no matter how big or small, are psychological suppositions. There may be some facts to support the actual occurrence of wars, but the aggressor is the one who is shortsighted and holds the false belief that conflicts can be resolved through fighting and benefits received through the use of brutal force. If one thoroughly observes human history and gains a mature view, one will easily recognize that the so-called "necessity of survival" is in truth not a necessity for fighting, but rather a matter related to human development.

For example, when children fight each other for candy, although candy may be a reason for fighting, it is a matter of individual development rather than a matter of survival. In the long run, wars and fighting among adults and nations are not the answer to survival. The survival of humanity can be achieved only through the avoidance of destruction.

The universal, integral spiritual teachings are mostly concerned with the growth and development of the individual human being. With regard to human society as a whole, the principle of "non-action" may be considered the guideline for a safe and peaceful future. For individual development, the ancient spiritual teachings may be summarized as follows:

If a person attempts to understand the phenomena of the universe without integrating the entirety of the fragmented facts, following only a single fact would cause loss of self. Whoever does this leaves one's true nature. Despite gathering superficial information about the world, he becomes a stranger to himself and inevitably misses the mark. To reach and touch all aspects of one's being, it is only necessary to dissolve the barrier between one's developed mind and one's already existing spiritual ability. This is the way to recognize and realize the truth of the universe, achieve completion of one's being and enjoy harmony in the eternally changing universe. Life and death are just like night and day. In a general sense, they are a necessary and the natural phenomena of movement.

Worldly people of ancient times interpreted the spiritual energy of the universe as gods or spirits. Those interpretations limited the spiritual energy by personalizing and making it rigid. The ancient sages recognized that spiritual energy is impersonal even while it takes form and becomes personalized. At the same time it is formed, it can also remain formless and beyond all concepts of personalization. The freedom of spiritual energy is complete and absolute. The entire universe is an integrated entity because of the existence of spiritual energy. The impersonal spiritual realm which is referred to as 'Heaven' or spirit, contains within it the personal physical realm, the physical body, which is referred to as 'earth,' and the mind, which is referred to as 'humankind.' Every human being contains the realms of Heaven and Earth, and their harmonization. Thus, the three spheres of universal energy transformation are inseparable, and the integrity of the universe is absolute.

When a human does not refine and cultivate himself, his or her energy remains on a heavy, adulterated and incomplete level. Hence he or she must accept the limitations of that plane of existence. However, because human beings possess highly developed sensitivity and intuition, they are able to cultivate energy and recognize the spiritual energy within their being as their center.

One way to keep the highest spiritual energy dwelling within oneself is to live a normal, peaceful and balanced life. Spiritual energy will reside firmly within the person who lives calmly and quietly, and harmonizes the three spheres of energy. Thus one may enjoy the integrity of one's true being.

In order to achieve the highest self-awareness and enlightenment through one's daily practices, one must keep one's spirit solitary and independent of the worldly environment. One needs to withdraw periodically from the noisy world each day, month and year, but for the completion of one's spiritual evolution, one must stay in the world and serve one's fellow men and women. This is how a practitioner of the Integral Way lives.

At the present time, the world needs new sages to initiate and accomplish the integration of humanity. It is necessary to simplify and humanize complicated social structures existing in today's world, and to regulate technological development to effect a balanced social evolution of humankind.

Integral medicine, for example, has proven itself through thousands of years of clinical experience and may be applied together with modern medicine, which can at times provide better explanations on certain levels through scientific devices. Furthermore, by studying the *I Ching*, one may come to really understand the universal movement, and through the teachings of Lao Tzu, one may come to really understand the truth of human historical development.

All these spiritual teachings, including the knowledge of the universal law of subtle energy response and the principle of appropriateness, which was also handed down through the ancient tradition, will provide the new world with the necessary wisdom and understanding to reach the goal of peace and happiness.

Afterword

When Tao is approached as a subject to be studied and comprehended by the human mind, three main aspects are discerned: the mystical, intuitional and philosophical Tao. The mystical Tao can only be realized through the practice of spiritual cultivation. It is the individual's spiritual experience and is completely beyond verbal description. The intuitional Tao is also beyond intellectual comprehension and can perceived only with an absolutely clear mind. The Masters transmit their spiritual and mental energy directly and nonverbally to their students and in this way awaken their internal subtle energy. If a student develops his intuition well, he is able to absorb the Master's energy and will reach enlightenment through his Master.

The philosophical Tao can be understood and studied intellectually. Through discourses with the Master and reading good spiritual literature, one can come to know Tao intellectually. Strictly speaking, Tao is neither a religion nor a philosophy, but since ancient times the Masters adopted the vehicle of religion or philosophy to instruct students. The actual intention of their teachings, however, is the dissolution of the barrier of language and thought, and the restoration of their student's integral being.

Thus, if you wish the complete development of your being, and a real education and enhancement of your talents, you will find that self-cultivation serves this purpose. You are the only one in the world who knows where you have an itch or a pain. Especially on the mental and spiritual levels, one's education or development becomes a very delicate subject. During the long process of your cultivation, various needs will arise and there is no one who knows your needs better than you. For this simple reason, integral spiritual education emphasizes self-cultivation and differs greatly from our contemporary educational system. The general education one receives in public schools today resembles ready-made clothes and shoes and is not designed to suit each person individually. Since the differences in the inner being or spirit of humans is much larger than those on the physical level, one can understand the importance of spiritual cultivation being on an individual basis.

Through the integral cultivation of the physical, mental and spiritual aspects of one's being, one may gain direct knowledge of the subtle universal law. The universal subtle law can be approached scientifically; it can be accurately applied to the realm of physics or discussed philosophically. Yet it is not merely the exploration of ideas. Direct knowledge of the universal subtle law is achieved through the development of pure insight, as it is realized by Masters of all ages who have the same abilities and make the same discoveries.

In order to benefit from the development of one's spiritual abilities, one must achieve the full cooperation of one's body, emotions and mind, and in this way evolve a balanced, virtuous being. My sincere wish is that the material presented in this book will enhance the reader's integral development and lead him on the way to the discovery of Tao.

Ni, Hua-Ching
November 1979
Los Angeles

The Spiritual Background of
The Union of Tao and Man

"In the tenth moon plum-blossoms bloom,
Awaiting the early arrival of the spring
If inanimate things can predict nature's Way
It would be folly for us not to follow the Tao."
(Lu, Tung Ping)

The spiritual roots of the "Union of Tao and Man" can be traced back to prehistoric times. The Chinese believe that before Emperor Fu Shi, who is said to have reigned around 8,000 years ago, the Earth was inhabited by gods. These supernatural beings came into existence as the result of the combination of the subtle, creative energy of the universe with the pure, physical energy of the Earth. These gods lived spontaneously and intuitively in perfect harmony with nature and had no need of any method of self-cultivation or restoration. Their lives were manifestations of pure natural law.

The period after Fu Shi until the end of the reign of the great Emperor Yu (2205-2125 B.C.) was known as the age of the semi-gods. During this period, the Emperors were profoundly spiritual and wise people who were deeply involved in researching and practicing esoteric methods which would restore their divine quality. Fu Shi is attributed with the discovery of the eight manifestations of the *I Ching*; the famous Yellow Emperor, Huang Ti (2697-2597 B.C.), was the author of the classic on internal medicine; and the great Emperors Niao (2357-2258 B.C.) and Shun (2255-2208), all practiced and handed down the Sacred Method until the reign of the son of Emperor Chih (2125-2116 B.C.). The Emperor Chih was the first to inherit the throne through family succession, whereas previously it has been passed only to sages. Those who succeeded Emperor

Chih were unable to attain the heavenly qualities of sages, so the age of the semi-gods came to an end.

Then came an era of leaders who were not spiritually developed. In this era, the Sacred Method was no longer handed down by Emperors but was transmitted generation after generation by inspired sages called shiens who lived in high mountains as hermits, apart from the masses who abused themselves through their life style. These enlightened people lived simply, in harmony with nature, and enjoyed the unceasing regenerative power of the universe. Sometimes shiens would come to live among people, but they generally went unrecognized because they hid their great wisdom and miraculous powers. Sometimes they traveled throughout the countryside helping people in need. Most of them, however, chose to reside quietly in the remote mountains far from the tumult of the world.

> *To attain Tao,*
> *It is not necessary*
> *   to go to the mountains.*
> *Stay right here.*
> *In the red dust, riding a golden horse -*
> *   there is a great practitioner of Tao.*
> *Thus it is said*
> *   the mountains provide only quietude.*
>   (Lu, Tung Ping)

Prior to the Han dynasty (206 B.C.-219 A.D.) the teaching of Tao was a pure spiritual tradition involved with restoring the divine nature of human beings through the cultivation of Tao, and was studied and practiced only by shiens and their disciples in the high mountains. These shiens were the forefathers of my tradition, the "Union of Tao and Man." Close to the end of the Han dynasty (c. 184 A.D.) a local religious cult, "The Yellow Hood" which also called itself Taoism, appeared. Several such cults existed in different ages. However, those religious movements must not be confused with the pure, spiritual tradition of ancient

Taoism which I call the Integral Way. They must never be mistaken for the ancient teaching of the high shiens.

> *What is Tao?*
> *It is just this.*
> *It cannot be rendered into speech.*
> *If you insist on an explanation,*
> *This means exactly this.* (Lu, Tung Ping)

One of the most famous shiens at the end of the Han dynasty was Kou Hong (205 A.D.). Inspired by his immortal grand-uncle, he went to Tien Tai Mountain in Chekiang Province to practice the secret formula of sublimation and refinement. He authored the book *Pao Po Tzu*, a collection of all the methods of self-cultivation in existence at that time. The theoretical part of his work has been translated into English. He succeeded in his cultivation and became an Immortal. In the same mountains, but in the Tang dynasty (618-906 A.D.), the Master Sz Ma Chung Jen, the author of *The Theory of Sitting, Forgetting and Uniting*, and his teacher, known as "The Son of Invisible Heaven," who authored a book of this title, both cultivated themselves and practiced the Sacred Method.

> *The elixir of immortality:*
> *There is no need to beg from others.*
> *The eight trigrams,*
> *The nine colors*
> *Are all on your palms.*
> *The five elementary formations,*
> *The four figures of the diagrams,*
> *All are within you.*
> *Understanding this*
> *You can communicate with the spirits.* (Lu, Tung Ping)

All of the famous "Eight Immortals" are descendants of the sacred tradition of the "Union of Tao and Man." The most famous of them is Master Lu, Tung Ping, who lived during the Tang dynasty and whose poems are quoted herein. The story of Lu, Tung Ping's enlightenment is contained in the famous play of the Yuan dynasty entitled the Yellow Millet Dream. This play depicts Lu, Tung Ping as a scholar traveling to the capital to take the court examination in hope of becoming appointed to a government position. He stopped one evening at a roadside inn where, while he was waiting for his supper of yellow millet to be cooked, he fell asleep. He dreamt that he went through many distressing circumstances until the finally met Chung-Li Ch'uan, who opened his eyes to the truth. Upon his awakening from the dream, eighty years of life experience had already passed.

Master Lu lived during the period of Chinese history when Buddhism was starting to flourish in China. He departed from the typical monastic custom of avoiding the people of the world and traveled around the country teaching the truth of immortal life.

People may sit until the cushion is worn through,
But never quite know the real Truth;
Let me tell you about the ultimate Tao:
It is here, enshrined within us. (Lu, Tung Ping)

Master Lu's disciple Leao Hai Chan, was the Premier to the Emperor Yen (c. 911 A.D.). Leao Hai Chan passed the Sacred Method to Shueh Bau Guan, who passed it to Shih Sing Ling, who passed it to Bai Yu Chan. These five shiens are called the "Five Forefathers of the Southern Branch."

Close your eyes to seek the Truth
And Truth comes naturally.
The pearl of Tao emits liveliness.
Play with it day and night,
And never throw it away
Lest the God of the Netherworld
Send his underlings after you. (Lu, Tung Ping)

I myself am a descendant of the shiens of Tien Tai Mountain, where Kou Hung refined his elixir of immortality. The Taoist temple in Tien Tai Mountain was built in memory of the enlightenment of the Taoist Prince Tung Pa, the son of Emperor Ling Wang (571-543 B.C.) of the Chou dynasty. Master Sz Ma Chung Jen of the Tang dynasty (618-906 A.D.) is the remote spiritual heir of Master Dao Hong-Cheng of the Chen dynasty (265-588 A.D.). Both, he and Master Jang Tse Yang of the Sung dynasty (960-1276 A.D.) cultivated in Tien Tai Mountain, and were part of the Southern Branch.

The Northern, Western and Eastern Branches were all formed separately. The Northern Branch started during the Yuan dynasty (1277-1367 A.D.) with Wang Jung Yang, who tried to preserve the Chinese from destruction by the invading Mongols. The most striking difference between this branch and the others is their strict practice of independent cultivation with celibacy for the novice. The Western and Eastern Branches were formed during the Ming dynasty (1368-1644 A.D.) and Ching dynasty (1644-1912 A.D.), respectively. Both schools share the same truths, the only difference being in a few secret techniques of cultivation.

Some of the Masters of the sacred family of shiens which constitute my lineage are:

Master Shih Ga or "Stone Drum" - his name comes from the practice of engraving mystical pictographs in stone; he lived in the Da Lu Mountains in Shueh-An County of Chekiang Province;

Master Shih Je or "Stone Disaster" - his name comes from his liking to break stones with his forehead; he lived in the South Yen Tang Mountains in Ping Yang County of Chekiang Province;

Master Tai Huang or "Great Wilderness" - who lived in the Da Lu Mountains;

Master Wei Feng or "Revolving Peak" - his name comes from the fact that the wild geese on their journey south or north would circle around the peak of the mountain he lived on in the North Yen Tang Mountains;

Master Teah Yuhn or "Crown of Strength" - his name depicts his strong virtues; he lived in the Mao Mountains in Chu Yung County of Kuansu Province;

Master Tung Yuhn or "Purple Clouds" - his name comes from the appearance of purple clouds in the sky at the time he achieved enlightenment; he is the author's father and lived in Chekiang Province; he practiced ancient Taoism (the Integral Way) and integral medicine;

Master Yen Tang Yin Jung or the "Hermit of Yen Tang;"

Master Tai Ruh Yin Yung or the "Hermit of Tai Ruh;"

Master Da Tao Tzu or the "Son of the Eternal Tao" - he is the author, Ni, Hua-Ching.

> *Sojourning in the Ta-Yu Mountains,*
> *Who converses with the white crane*
> *That comes flying?*
> *How many times have the mountain people*
> *Seen the winter plum-flowers blossoming.*
> *Spring comes and goes,*
> *Deep in fallen flowers and streams.*
> *People are not aware*
> *Of the many Immortals around them.* (Lu, Tung Ping)

Appendix

The Ancient Integral View of the Organs

The ancient achieved ones categorized six of the twelve energy spheres of the body as yin and six as yang, based on the principles of yin and yang and the five phases of energy evolution. Each of the five phases of energy evolution controls one yin sphere and one yang sphere, except the fire phase, which controls two. The energy spheres naturally fall into two groups: the fu spheres, which correspond with the yang channels, and the zhang spheres, which correspond with the yin channels. The fus are considered yang spheres because they are concerned with the activity of transforming, transporting, and expelling material ingested from external sources (i.e., food). The fus transform food but do not store anything, and become most active when full. The zhangs are considered yin spheres because they have the relatively passive role of holding and storing energy (i.e., life essence). Zhang translated literally means "storage bin." The zhangs transform the energy derived from food and air to a form which may nourish the body. The fu spheres are the gall bladder, the stomach, the small intestine, the large intestine, the bladder, and the triple warmer. The zhang spheres are the heart, the pericardium, the liver, the spleen (which also includes some of the physiological functions of the anatomical organ pancreas), the kidneys and the lungs.

The zhang and fu spheres function within the body in pairs, with one zhang sphere as the yin polarity of one phase in the cycle of energy evolution, and one fu sphere as its complementary yang polarity. Ideally, the spheres function in an alternating manner; when the stomach is filled, the intestines are empty, and vice versa. They are alternately filled and emptied so that the energy is able to ascend and descend.

The relationship between the zhangs and fus is also that of mutual creating and controlling, according to the principle of the five phases of energy evolution. The zhang and fu spheres are interdependent. The fus need the zhangs spheres to provide them with the transformed energy from food, and the zhangs need the energy from the fus to perform their own work of energy transformation. The primary function of the zhang and fu spheres is the processing of energy and manufacturing of blood for the body. Although the zhangs are classified as yin and the fus as yang, of course both contain a composite of yin and yang activities. Physiologically, this duality of yin and yang functions within all organ is quite obvious: the heart contracts and expands, accelerates or slows down, the lungs inhale and exhale, the liver stores and releases, the kidneys absorb and secrete, the spleen/pancreas secrete both insulin and glucagon. (Glucagon is a hormone which is an antagonist of insulin.)

Because each organ sphere is a functional representation within the body of a specific phase in the cosmic cycle of energy evolution, the definition of a sphere includes the corresponding relationships with all the other manifestations of that phase existing in the universe. Thus, in its interaction with the macrocosm, each organ sphere corresponds with a certain planet in the solar system, a certain time of day (the position of the sun and moon), a certain direction, a certain climatic energy manifestation, and has an affinity to a certain season. Each organ sphere corresponds with specific sensory data: with a certain flavor, color, or smell, a certain musical tone according to the Chinese five tone scale, and more generally, with the sound of a particular musical instrument. Each organ sphere corresponds with one of the five senses. Each sphere has a corresponding cereal which is especially nourishing to the energy of the sphere. A particular emotional reaction to the external environment is associated with each sphere and is generated by the energy of that sphere. Each sphere also has its own vocal manifestation of emotions and feelings.

In its interaction with the microcosm, each sphere is paired with another sphere of the same phase but of complementary polarity. For example, the lung sphere, which is metal of yin polarity, is paired with the large intestine sphere, which is metal of yang polarity. Each organ sphere has a corresponding cardinal channel and a specific radial pulse which indicates the functional condition of the organ sphere. Each organ sphere has another sphere which counteracts or controls its activity according to the checking sequence of the five phases of energy evolution. Each zhang sphere manifests its energy as various other anatomical entities. The nervous system, for example, is a manifestation of the energy of the liver sphere. Each zhang sphere has a corresponding sense organ and body opening, and each organ sphere has its own related bodily secretion which frequently accompanies the emotional reaction.

If the energy of a sphere is out of harmony with the functions of the other spheres, specific themes may appear in the dreams of the individual which would indicate this disturbance. And finally, with the exception of the triple warmer, each organ has an anatomical correspondence.

The Zhang (yin) Spheres
The Heart (Shin)

> *The heart (Shin) is the supreme Master of the organs and is the residence of the essence and spirit.*
> (Su Wen)

The heart sphere is the control center of the body and includes in its realm the invisible mind and the visible organ, the heart. It is considered the "sovereign ruler" of the body because it is the residence of the "directing energy" called shen, the spirit or divine energy of the individual, which participates in and regulates the activities of all the other spheres of the entire being. The heart sphere functions to direct the working of the blood vessels and the pulses. It also functions to integrate all aspects of the organism, including all facets of the personality. When the energy of this sphere ascends upward to the brain, it functions as the mind. When it descends downward to the organs, it functions as the balancing center of the organism.

Both the mind and heart sphere correspond with the five phases of energy evolution. Bitter is the corresponding flavor of the heart sphere, scarlet is its color, and the scorched smell is its corresponding odor. The tone chih corresponds with it and the sound of the thirty-six reed mouth organ. The heart and mind correspond with the faculty of speech. The domestic animal which corresponds with the heart is the energy of sheep and the cereal energy is yellow millet. The early understanding of these correspondences is the ancient predecessor of the recent application of diet, color and music in therapy.

The emotion which corresponds with the heart sphere is joy or pleasure. Laughter is its corresponding vocal expression. Joy and laughter stimulate the energy of the heart, yet in excess will tend to exhaust it. If the energy of the heart sphere is disturbed, this may express itself in the following dream themes: "If the energy in the heart is exhausted, in dreams one will look for fire and yang things. At the right moment one even dreams of fire and blazes," (*Nei Ching*). The right moment refers to the two hour time period when the energy in the heart sphere reaches its peak. "If the heart energy is abundant, one easily laughs in dreams or is afraid; or one may see blazing flames. If there is an acute deficiency of energy in the heart, in one's dreams there appear hills of ashes and gray mountains." (*Ling-Shu*)

As it relates to the macrocosm, the summer season corresponds with the heart, as does the southern direction. Its corresponding climate is heat. The planet Mars corresponds with the heart. According to the yearly energy cycle, the energy is most concentrated in the heart sphere during the fifth and sixth months of the integrated solar and lunar calendar, approximately in June and July. According to the daily energy cycle, it is between the hours of 11 a.m. and 1 p.m. These cycles are usually referred to as the body's natural clock.

Diseases of the heart sphere, which includes the mind and the anatomical organ of the heart, tend to produce the following symptoms: fearfulness, trembling in the heart, insomnia, general restlessness, mumbling to oneself, dizziness and fainting spells, excessive sadness, or sometimes raucous, incessant laughter. Because the heart sphere is the master of the other spheres, any disease affecting it will quickly disturb all other functions. The classics say: "If the Master is brilliant, his subjects are peaceful. If the Master is disturbed, then his twelve officials are in danger."

The Pericardium Sphere

The pericardium sphere is the official ambassador of the heart sphere and is the origin of joy and sadness. (Su Wen)

The pericardium sphere has two functions: to protect the heart sphere and to maintain the order of its energy. The pericardium is also the reservoir of the energy entrusted to the individual at birth. The anatomical correspondence of the pericardium sphere is the fatty membrane which encases the heart. Like the heart sphere, the pericardium corresponds with the fire phase in the cycle of energy evolution. Yet whereas the heart and its paired sphere, the small intestine, are known as the "princely fire," the pericardium and its paired sphere, the triple warmer, are known as the "ministerial fire." All of the fire spheres share the same general correspondences according to the five phases of energy evolution.

Disease of the pericardium sphere is evidenced by symptoms of dizziness, loss of voice, delirium and fever.

The Liver Sphere

The liver sphere is considered "the general" within the organism because it is in charge of the defense strategy of the body. The main functions of the liver are to cleanse and regulate the supply of blood to the body and to maintain the body's defense mechanism. The activity of defense is carried out by storing and releasing the defense energies of the body. When sickness attacks the body, the defense energies and the blood are roused into activity.

The liver also regulates the functions of the nervous system. When a person is easily fatigued, it indicates that his liver energy is depleted and must be restored by food and rest.

The liver sphere corresponds with the wood phase in the cycle of energy evolution. The sour flavor corresponds with the liver, as does the color green and the smell of urine. Its corresponding sound is the tone chio and the sound of the lute. The sense of sight is its corresponding sense. The domestic animal which corresponds with the liver is the energy of the chicken, and its corresponding cereal is wheat.

The paired yang sphere of the liver is the gall bladder. The sphere responsible for controlling the activity of the liver is the lung sphere. The extension of the energy of the liver sphere within the body is the nervous system. The liver outwardly manifests itself in the nails. The specific body opening and the corresponding senses are the eyes. By observing the appearance of the nails and the sharpness of sight, one may gather information about the functional condition of this sphere. Tears are the secreted fluid which is a manifestation of the energy of the liver.

The emotion corresponding to the liver is anger. Shouting is its corresponding vocal expression. If liver energy is exhausted, one will be overcome by fear; if it is excessive, by anger. If the energy of the liver is disturbed, it may be expressed in the following dream topics: "If liver energy is exhausted, in dreams one will see mushrooms; at the right moment one has the sensation of lying under a tree and not daring to get up." (*Nei-ching*) "If the energy is deficient and the direction of its flow is hence reversed, one dreams of trees in a mountain forest." (*Ling-shu*)

The vision and content of a patient's dream can often be used as a valuable component in making correct diagnosis, because dreams frequently reveal the nature of disturbances in body, mind and spirit.

As it relates to the macrocosm, the liver corresponds with spring and the eastern direction. Its corresponding climatic energy manifestation is wind, and its planet is Jupiter. According to the yearly energy cycle, the energy is most concentrated in the liver sphere during the first and second lunar months, approximately in March. Energy becomes stronger when it moves to a new solar cycle starting over again by Aries (the first section of the zodiac). According to the daily cycle, the strong time is between the hours of 1 a.m. and 3 a.m.

Diseases of the liver sphere tend to produce the following symptoms: headaches, dizziness, redness of face and eyes, blurred vision, glaucoma and soft, ridged nails.

The Spleen Sphere
The ancient integral medical system, which was developed through pure insight into the human body as a living entity, can supply information about the actual condition of the energy flow. It is not dependent on information gathered from anatomically dissected body parts and the chemical analysis of separated, isolated components. This fundamental difference in the approach to the human body brought about the difference in the development of integral and western medicine.

In the integral medical system, the sphere referred to as the spleen includes functions which according to western physiology are attributed to the pancreas. In the integral system, these two organs are regarded as being interlinked and acting almost as one organ, although only one organ is named. Thus, bear in mind that when the spleen is referred to, the pancreas is also included.

The primary function of the spleen sphere is to control the transformation, distribution and storage of nourishment and energy for the entire body. Food in its undigested form cannot be utilized as nourishment for the body. Both its chemical and energetic construction must be altered to suit the body's requirements. The spleen works in conjunction with the stomach, its paired yang sphere, to perform this role. The *Su Wen* says: "Food enters the stomach and the essence is driven off and passes through the spleen. The energy of the spleen transforms the essence, which then rises to the lungs." The spleen also transforms the liquid from food and distributes it to the other organs for absorption. The physiological function of the spleen is the regulation of blood volume. It stores the nourishing energy of the body called ying chi, and has an essential role in both memory and imagination.

The spleen corresponds with the earth phase of energy evolution. The flavor corresponding to the spleen is sweet; the color is yellow; the smell is fragrant. The tone kung and the sound of the drum are its corresponding sounds. The domestic animal which corresponds with the spleen is the energy of the ox and the cereal is rye.

The sphere responsible for controlling the activity of the spleen is the liver sphere. The extension of the energy of the spleen is the flesh and its outward manifestation is the lips. Its corresponding body opening is the mouth and its sense organ is the tongue. The sense organ of the heart sphere is also the tongue, and the *Ling-Shu* makes the following distinction: "If the energy of the heart sphere is in harmony, the tongue may distinctly perceive the five flavors. If the energy of the spleen sphere is in harmony, the tongue may perceive whether food is palatable." Saliva is a manifestation of the energy of the spleen.

The emotion which corresponds with the spleen is deep thinking, pondering or reminiscence. Singing is its vocal manifestation. If the energy of the spleen is disturbed, this may be expressed in the following dream topics: "If the energy of the spleen is exhausted, one dreams of lacking food and drink. At the right moment one dreams of erecting walls and buildings," (*Nei Ching*). "If the energy is abundant in the spleen, one dreams that one chants and plays music, yet one's body is heavy and one cannot rise. If acute deficiency of energy exists, in one's dreams there appear hills and marshes, ruined buildings and storms." (*Ling-Shu*)

As the spleen relates to the macrocosm, Indian summer is its corresponding season and the central position its direction. Its corresponding climate is humidity. The planet Saturn is its corresponding planet. According to the yearly energy cycle, the energy is most concentrated in the spleen during the third and fourth lunar months, approximately in April and May, and according to the daily energy cycle, between the hours of 9 and 11 a.m.

Diseases of the spleen tend to produce the following symptoms: digestive problems, lack of appetite, diarrhea, and tiredness.

The Lung Sphere
Within the organism, the lung sphere holds the office of "minister" on whom rhythmic order depends. It represents the sphere of respiratory function, which influences not only the rhythm of the pulse but all energetic processes in the body as well. A commentary in one of the medical classics states: "The lung sphere controls breathing and chi. If the breathing is in rhythmic harmony, then the nourishing and defensive energies (yeng and wei) and all the organ spheres are in good order." The breath and chi are both vital factors in human life. The lungs also control the function of the skin and pores.

The lungs correspond with the metal phase of energy evolution. The hot flavor corresponds with it, as does the color white and the fleshy smell of raw meat or fish. The tone shang and the sound of resonant stones are its corresponding sounds. The domestic animal which corresponds with the lungs is the energy of the horse and its cereal is rice.

The paired yang sphere of the lungs is the large intestine. The sphere responsible for controlling the activity of the lungs is the heart. The extension of the energy of the lungs is the skin and its external manifestation is body hair. Their appearance permits inferences to be drawn on the general condition of the lungs. The corresponding body opening as well as its sense organ is the nose. Consequently the bodily fluid which corresponds with the lungs is the mucous secreted by the nose.

The emotion which corresponds with the lungs is sorrow or grief. Weeping is its corresponding vocal expression. If the energy of the lungs is disturbed, this may be expressed in the following dream themes: "If the energy of the lungs is exhausted, this causes white objects to appear in dreams, or cruel killing people," (*Nei Ching*). White is the symbolic color of west and of metal and is therefore associated with weapons; it is also the color of mourning. "If there is an excess of energy in the lungs one will be frightened in dreams, cry, or soar through the air. If there is an extreme deficiency of lung energy, one dreams of soaring through the air or sees strange objects made out of metal," (*Ling Shu*).

As it relates to the macrocosm, autumn corresponds with the lungs, as does the western direction. Its corresponding climate is dry weather. The planet Venus corresponds with the lungs. According to the yearly energy cycle, the energy is most concentrated in the lungs during the seventh and eighth lunar months, approximately in August and September, and according to the daily energy cycle, between the hours of 3 and 5 a.m.

The Kidney Sphere
The kidney sphere has two functions: to control fluid in the body and to store essence. There are two kinds of essence which the kidneys store. The first is the essence of the zhang and fu spheres which is derived from food and air and is the basic nourishment of life. This can be released on demand to any organ sphere. The second kind of essence which the kidneys store is reproductive essence, the basic substances of human reproduction. These essences are formed from the action of the pre-natal energy (yuan chi) on the energy refined from food (ching chi).

The kidneys correspond with the water phase of energy evolution. The salty flavor corresponds, as does the color black and the decaying odor. The tone yu and the sound of the twenty-five stringed lute are its corresponding sounds. The kidneys correspond with the sense of hearing. The domestic animal which corresponds with the kidneys is the energy of pigs and the corresponding cereal is beans.

The paired yang sphere of the kidneys is the bladder. The sphere responsible for controlling the activity of the kidneys is the spleen. The extension of the energy of the kidneys within the body is the bone and marrow. The kidneys outwardly manifest their energy in the hair of the head. The corresponding body openings are the urethra and the anus and the sense organ is the ears. The bodily fluid which is a manifestation of the kidney energy is urine.

The emotion which corresponds with the kidneys is fear. Groaning is its corresponding vocal expression. If the energy of the kidneys is disturbed, this may be expressed in the following dream themes: "If the energy of the kidneys is exhausted, this causes ships and boats and drowning men to appear in one's dreams. At the right time one dreams of lying in the water and becomes frightened," (Nei Ching). "If there is an excess of energy in the kidneys, in dreaming one has the sensation that the back and waist are split apart and can no longer be stretched. If an extreme depletion exists, one dreams of approaching a ravine, plunging into water, or being in the water," (Ling-Shu). As it relates to the macrocosm, winter corresponds with the kidneys, as does the northern direction. Its corresponding climate is bitter cold. The planet Mercury corresponds with the kidneys. According to the yearly energy cycle, the energy is most concentrated in the kidney sphere during the tenth and eleventh lunar months, approximately in November and December, and according to the daily energy cycle, between the hours of 5 and 7 p.m.

Diseases of the kidneys tend to produce the following symptoms: sexual disorders, irregular menstruation, deterioration of the bones, lumbago, weak extremities, impaired hearing and forgetfulness.

The Fu (yang) Spheres

The Gall Bladder Sphere

The gall bladder sphere influences the circulation of the nourishing and protective energies of the body (ying and wei). The *Su-Wen* says: "Although the nourishing and protective energies are controlled by the lungs, their circulation is controlled by the gall bladder." The gall bladder is the only fu which transforms and stores energies in a manner similar to a zhang. All the other fu spheres are concerned with the transportation of refined and unrefined liquids and solids. The gall bladder is the only yang sphere with refined contents. It is also the only yang sphere that participates in the assimilation of food but not in its ingestion and transportation.

The gall bladder is titled the "minister of justice" within the organism and directs the impulses of all the other organs. The classics assign the ability to plan to the liver and the ability to decide to the gall bladder. It is only when both organs are equally healthy that an individual may demonstrate courage and decisiveness.

The gall bladder corresponds with the wood phase of energy evolution. Its paired sphere is the liver; thus, it shares the liver's same general correspondences. A disturbance of gall bladder energy may express itself in the following dream themes: "If an extreme deficiency exists in the gall bladder, one dreams of being engaged in fights and battles or that one cuts open one's own body," (*Nei Ching*).

The Stomach Sphere

The stomach sphere is referred to as the "sea of nourishment." The *Nei Ching* says: "The stomach is the sea of the zhang and fus, food comes to them via the stomach so the stomach is their sea of energy." The stomach sphere governs digestion. The spleen, which is its paired sphere, is in charge of distributing and circulating the essences from the food. Because of the stomach's central position and the importance of its role as the depository of nourishment for the body, any disease of the stomach will quickly reflect in the other spheres. If its function collapses completely, as diagnosed by the absence of its corresponding pulse, this is interpreted as a sure sign of immanent death.

The stomach corresponds with the earth phase in the cycle of energy evolution. It shares the same general correspondences as its paired sphere, the spleen. A disturbance of the stomach energy may be expressed in the following dream themes: "If an extreme deficiency exists in the stomach energy, one dreams of eating and drinking," (*Ling-Shu*).

The Large Intestine Sphere
The large intestine functions as a conduit in which the assimilation and the passage of food residues take place. It is in charge of transporting and transforming the residue from food.

The large intestine corresponds with the metal phase in the cycle of energy evolution. It is paired with the lung sphere and shares its general correspondences. If the energy of the large intestine is disturbed, it may be expressed in the following dream themes: "If an extreme deficiency in the large intestine exists, one dreams of fields and rural landscapes" (*Ling-Shu*).

The Bladder Sphere
The *Nei Ching* says: "The bladder is the provincial officer in charge of liquids." All the excess fluids of the body convene and are stored in the bladder. Some of this excess will be evaporated as sweat or passed out with the feces, but most will descend to the bladder for evacuation.

The bladder corresponds with the water phase in the cycle of energy evolution. It is paired with the kidney sphere and shares its general correspondences. If the bladder energy is disturbed, it may express itself in the following dream themes: "If an extreme deficiency of energy in the bladder exists, in dreams one takes walks and excursions," (*Ling-Shu*)

The Small Intestine Sphere
The *Nei Ching* says: "The small intestines are the receiver vessels (of food) and assimilation occurs here." The function of the small intestines is to receive digested food from the stomach and to process it further. In the small intestines, the coarser elements of the food are separated from the fine and the nourishing liquid from the food is absorbed. The small intestines then pass the residue to the large intestine.

The small intestines correspond with the fire phase in the cycle of energy evolution. They share the same general correspondences with the heart sphere, which is its paired sphere. If the energy of the small intestines is disturbed, this may be evidenced by the following dream theme: "If an extreme deficiency of energy exists within the small intestines, one will dream of populous town districts and of main thoroughfares." (*Ling-Shu*)

The Triple Warmer Sphere
The triple warmer is not a single organ, but rather a group of physiological functions involving three groups of organs. The upper warmer involves the lungs and the heart; the middle warmer involves the stomach, the spleen and the liver; and the lower warmer involves the kidneys, the large and small intestines, and the bladder. Although the triple warmer does not have a separate organ, its energy network extends through the membranes of the body cavities. The membranes combined with the fat deposits provide a protection for the organs and regulate the body temperature. The triple warmer holds and adjusts the heat necessary for the various processes of energy transformation which take place in the body. It also influences the supply of blood, chi, and fluids for the muscles, skin and the other eleven organ spheres. It does not directly participate in the work of the digestion, assimilation and excretion of food by the stomach, spleen and intestines, yet it is involved with the regulation of the body's energy spheres in the form of thermal energy circulation, which flows parallel to the circulation of blood

and other liquid energies. The triple warmer is the source of protective energy or wei chi.

Diseases with dangerously high fevers relate to a malfunction of the membranes (of the brain) and the triple warmer. If the membranes are constricted, the energy flow is impeded and the heat will build inside the trunk of the body. This may result in an upward pressure and manifest as an inflammation of the throat or the gums. Or it may result in downward pressure, as for example in brief, yellow and hot urination. If a person has weak energy, the membranes will not be able to retain the body heat well enough. When the membranes are too tight, fever results, and when they are too loose, one will lack energy because all the organs need to be embraced by the warmth of the membranes.

The triple warmer corresponds with the fire phase in the cycle of energy evolution. Its paired organ is the pericardium and it shares the same general correspondences as the other three fire spheres.

About Hua-Ching Ni

The author, Hua-Ching Ni, feels that it is his responsibility to ensure that people receive his message clearly and correctly, thus, he puts the lectures and classes in book form from various occasions with the single purpose of universal spiritual unity.

It will be his great happiness to see the genuine progress of all people, all societies and nations as one big harmonious worldly community. This is the goal that makes him talk and write as one way of fulfilling his personal duty.

What he offers people comes from his own growth and attainment. He began his personal spiritual pursuit when he was ten years old. Although his spiritual nature is innate, expressing it suitably and usefully requires worldly experience and learning.

When he is asked to give personal information, he says that there is personally nothing useful or worthy of mention. He feels that, as an individual, he is just one person living on the same plane of life with the rest of humanity and therefore he is not special. A hard life and hard work have made him deeper and stronger, and perhaps wiser. This is the case with all people who do not yield to the negative influences of life and the world. He does not work to establish himself as a special individual as people in general spiritual society do.

He likes to be considered a friend rather than be formally titled, because he enjoys the natural spiritual response between himself and others who come together to extend the ageless natural spiritual truth to all.

He has been a great traveller. He has been in many places, and he never tires of going to new places. His books have been printed in different languages as a supplement to his professional work as a natural healer - a fully trained Traditional Chinese Medical doctor. He understands that his world mission is to awaken many people, and his friends and helpers as Mentors conjointly fulfill the world spiritual mission of this time.

INDEX

acupuncture 20, 36, 39, 41, 47, 53, 70
Alternation of Stillness and Movement 73
ancestors iv
art iii, 21, 36, 53, 83, 87, 121, 135
astral world v
attitudes 25, 78
aura 20
awakening 66, 142, 153
balance 3, 14, 26-29, 32-35, 39, 42, 54-56, 61, 63, 68, 73, 74, 77, 78, 80, 81, 83, 87, 93, 96, 104, 106, 141
bladder 37, 39, 156, 161, 166-169
Bladder Sphere 167, 168
blessings 124, 127
Body-Mind Integration 81
Book of Changes 8, 22, 135
Buddhism 153
business 138
calendar 112, 159
calmness 77, 86, 106, 116
cause and effect 132
celestial bodies v, vi
celibacy 154
centered 94, 104, 124, 127
channel 27-30, 36, 39, 41, 47, 77, 78, 85, 86, 108, 158
channels 28, 30, 31, 37-41, 51, 77, 78, 111, 119, 156
chi 1, 8-10, 25-27, 36, 44-52, 55, 59, 68, 69, 71-91, 111, 117, 135, 144, 163-165, 169, 170
ching chi 45, 46, 48, 49, 165
Chou Dynasty 154
Circularity of All Natural Movement 74
clarity vii, viii, 7, 28, 96, 104, 106, 124, 132
concentration 86
congestion 59
correspondences of yin and yang 7
crown 155

cycle 10, 11, 13, 14, 21-23, 40-42, 44, 67, 105, 156, 157, 159-162, 164-166, 168-170
Daily Living 116
dance 82
death 45, 46, 64, 72, 85, 117, 121, 132, 141, 146, 168
desire 105-107, 141
destiny vi, 23, 24, 102, 121
devotion 86
diagrams 103, 152
diet 49, 53, 55, 56, 60, 61, 64, 70, 159
discipline 27, 94-97, 99, 125
Divination 135, 136
dream 133, 134, 153, 159, 161, 163, 165-169
Dreaming 133, 161, 166
dreams 119, 133, 134, 158, 159, 161-168
education 148
ego 31, 141
eight great manifestations 10
eight treasures 111
Emotional Balance 56, 93, 104
emotions 21, 26, 30, 35, 56-58, 62-64, 70, 78, 92-95, 98, 113, 117, 149, 157
energy cycle 10, 11, 23, 40, 67, 159, 162, 164-166
energy flow 41, 64, 68, 70, 74, 77, 78, 81, 95, 111, 162, 170
Energy in Daily Life 24
Energy Manifestations within the Body 44
enlightenment 108, 147, 148, 153-155
Essential Principles for Practicing T'ai Chi Ch'uan 91
ethics iii, iv, 23, 101-103, 108
exercise 41, 53, 55, 59, 64, 66, 70, 73, 77, 79-82, 85, 87, 123
fame 142
fasting 118
First Stage 23
five elements 12, 21, 60

five phases 12-16, 20, 23, 25, 37, 39, 41, 42, 44, 54, 56, 60, 136, 156, 158-160
four seasons 22, 37, 44, 63, 121
freedom 30, 97, 108, 132, 146
Fu (Yang) Spheres 167
Fu Shi 4, 118, 150
gall bladder 39, 156, 161, 167
Gall Bladder Sphere 167
general guidelines 64
gentle movement 71
Gentle Path 85
Gentle Path T'ai Chi Movement 85
Gentle Rhythmic versus Hasty Violent Movements 74
geomancy 21, 137, 138
goals 33, 75
Good Deeds 129, 131
government position 153
Guidelines iii, iv, 63, 64, 101, 115
habits 20, 53, 64, 65, 70, 81, 116, 141
Han Dynasty 151, 152
happiness 25, 57, 64, 92, 94, 95, 98, 131, 132, 141, 147 158, 163, 164
healing 36, 38, 41-43, 53, 55, 70, 77
heart 25, 27, 37, 39, 45, 52, 56-58, 60, 62, 67, 68, 77, 79, 95, 115, 117, 118, 120, 132, 141, 156-160, 163, 164, 169
Heart (Shin) 158
Heaven 2, 3, 7, 8, 10, 45, 46, 63, 86, 118, 128, 132, 134, 137, 139, 146, 152
heavenly way 22
herbology 20
herbs 53, 70, 112
hermit 64, 155
hermit of the western mountain 64
hormones 23
host 55
humanity iii, vi, 128, 145, 147
hun 52, 72
I Ching 8, 11, 103, 135, 136, 147, 150
immortality 115, 124, 152, 154

immortals 152, 155
Infinite Expansion T'ai Chi movement 86
inspiration 105
Integral Healing 36, 38, 41-43
integral truth 112
integration 8, 72, 81-83, 86, 144, 147
internal alchemy 75, 86
intuition 7, 146, 148
invocation 123, 125, 134, 135
Invocations 111, 119, 123
jen mo 27, 28, 41
joy 25, 26, 35, 56, 57, 92, 99, 117, 159, 160
Kidney Sphere 48, 49, 52, 165, 166, 168
kidneys 37, 49, 54, 57, 58, 60, 68, 69, 156, 157, 165, 166, 169
Kou Hong 152
ku chi 46, 50
kua 8
Lao Tzu 75, 118, 121, 147
large intestine 37, 39, 156, 158, 164, 168, 169
Large Intestine Sphere 158, 168
Law of Reversion 75
law of yin and yang 41
laws v, 1, 4, 32-34, 37, 59, 71, 81, 132
Learning vi, 20, 33, 34, 84, 139
Lieh Tzu 113-115, 120, 121, 126, 129, 130, 133, 136, 140, 142, 143
light 9, 10, 32, 70, 89, 90, 97, 134, 144
liver 27, 37, 39, 45, 50, 52, 54, 57, 60, 61, 68, 69, 156, 157, 158, 160-163, 167, 169
Liver Sphere 52, 57, 158, 160-163
longevity 67, 141
love 56, 96-98, 117, 124, 126, 131
Lu, Tung Ping 150-153, 155
Lung Sphere 157, 161, 164, 168
magic vii, 118, 119
marriage 106, 138
martial arts 83

massage 65, 80
Master Lu 152, 153
Master Lu, Tung Ping 152
Master Zhan, San Fong 88
medicine 10, 20, 21, 26, 37, 43, 49, 53, 64, 147, 150, 155, 162
meditation 73, 74, 81, 93, 95, 109, 111
menopause 49
menstruation 26, 105, 166
mirror 25, 26
money 112, 119, 127
moon v, 5, 7, 36, 44, 105, 150, 157
music 65, 159, 163
natural life 46, 49, 55, 66
navel 46, 67, 85
Nei Ching 44, 45, 55, 57, 159, 163, 165-169
Niao 150
normalcy 98, 99
nothingness 2-4
orbit circulation 41
pancreas 37, 156, 157, 162
parents v, 49
peace vii, 34, 56, 64, 68, 97-99, 110, 141, 145, 147
pericardium 37, 39, 156, 160, 170
Pericardium Sphere 160
perineum 28
personality iii, vi, 22, 34, 35, 37, 52, 83, 84, 97, 98, 158
Personality Development 34, 83
pineal gland 79
planets 32, 44, 45, 59
po 51, 52, 72, 113, 114, 152
poisons 55
politics 96
positive thinking 83, 84
Power of Natural Healing 70
powers 7, 151
prayer 121, 122, 126, 127
Praying 121
preface iii
prejudice 109
Principle of Appropriateness 98, 100, 102, 108, 147

Principle of Appropriateness in Ethics 102
Principle of Energy Rotation 22
psychic energy 67
Psychological Health iii, 96
purification 119, 134
purity 124
Realization 87, 97, 111, 115, 124, 125
reason 31, 50, 66, 69, 94, 106, 145, 148
relationship v, 4, 36, 156
religions 121, 129
reputation 119, 130
Reverent Offerings 127
Sacred Method 118, 119, 150-153
San Han Luon 10
Second Stage 23
self-cultivation v, 26, 27, 29, 33, 79, 84, 95, 97, 98, 108, 109, 110-112, 124, 132, 148, 150, 152
self-discipline 27, 94-97, 99
self-healing 77
selfless service 132
sen 51
sensitivity vii, 27, 31, 85, 95, 105, 136, 138, 146
service 97, 112, 116, 127, 132
sex 27
sexual activity 48, 66, 110, 112
sexual energy 85
sexuality 85, 112
shen 51, 52, 58, 62, 72, 118, 158
Shen Nung 118
Shun 150
simplicity 28, 108, 113, 115, 124, 133, 137
sincerity 95, 122, 135
six basic soundless sounds 67, 70
Sky Journey 86
sleep 58, 66, 111
small intestine 37, 39, 156, 160, 169
Small Intestine Sphere 169
society vi, 29, 97, 98, 101, 104, 145
solar energy 11, 23
son 14, 150, 152, 154, 155

soul 51, 72, 117, 122, 131
spine 80, 89, 90
spirits 31, 82, 122, 134, 135, 146,
    152
spiritual cultivation 28, 84, 109,
    111, 113, 148, 149
spiritual development 131
Spleen Sphere 52, 162, 163
stars v, 36, 44
stomach 37, 39, 46, 50, 61, 65,
    68, 80, 156, 163, 167, 168,
    169
Stomach Sphere 167
strength iii, 46, 82, 83, 88, 91,
    96, 105, 116, 155
Su-Wen 2, 6, 12, 45, 53, 56, 57,
    61, 63, 167
sublimation 119, 152
subtle law 149
subtle light 70
subtle origin 2, 7, 8, 29, 32, 76,
    85, 125, 131, 135
subtle universal law 149
summer 7, 11, 22, 23, 54, 61, 62,
    65, 66, 85, 121, 159, 164
sun v, 3, 5, 7, 10, 32, 36, 44, 63,
    74, 78, 105, 157
Sung Dynasty 154
survival 144, 145
symmetry 32, 73, 87
T'ai Chi 8, 9, 48, 59, 71-88, 91,
    111, 144
t'ai chi movement 48, 59, 71, 72,
    74-87, 111
tai chi 80
Tai Mountain 152, 154
tan tien 46, 47, 67, 79, 85-87,
    104, 134
Tang Dynasty 152-154
Tao Teh Ching 28, 29, 75
temple 128, 154
thieves 139, 140
three circulations of life force 38
thymus 79
Tien Tai Mountain 152, 154
Treatise on T'ai Chi Chuan 88
Triple Warmer Sphere 46, 169
tu mo 27, 28, 41

Undivided Oneness is the Root of
    all Movement 71
unity 95
Universal Development 8
Universal Law of Subtle Energy
    Response iv, v, 100-102,
    130, 132, 147
Universal Principle of harmony,
    Order and Balance 32
vibration 1, 68, 69, 122, 144
vibrations 67, 68
virtue 34, 35, 71, 74, 96, 99,
    102-104, 124, 126, 132
vital energy 1, 25, 28, 36, 38, 43,
    45, 46, 80, 112
vitality 45, 47, 49, 52, 54, 59, 66,
    70, 73, 77, 89
wealth 140
wei chi 46-51, 170
well-being 23, 53, 70, 95, 109,
    116
Wisdom iv, 34, 85, 96, 99, 105,
    107, 116, 120, 135, 147, 151
work v, viii, 21, 43, 83, 92, 96,
    116, 136, 139, 152, 157, 169
worship 129
wu chi 73, 87
wu-hsing 2, 9, 12, 13, 20
Yellow Emperor 2, 4, 44, 47, 55,
    116-118, 150
yin and yang 2-7, 10, 28-30, 32,
    34, 35, 37, 39, 41, 42, 51,
    72, 73, 84, 87-89, 136, 137,
    139, 144, 156, 157
Yin and Yang and the Principle of
    Symmetry 73
Yin and Yang Principle in Behavior
    34
yin/yang 2, 20, 21, 103
yoga 109
yuan chi 45-47, 49, 51, 165
Yuan Dynasty 153, 154
Zhan, San Fong 88
Zhang (yin) Spheres 158
zodiac 162